I AM
The LIGHT

The Wisdom of Jesus in the 21st Century

Written and Channeled by
Patricia Horton
A Medium at Heart

We will all cross the great divide one day and leave a life well lived behind us. It does not mean that the life we lived no longer matters. It just means that we gave, learned, and grew while we were here. It is when our contract is fulfilled that God will call us home.

I Am the Light

The Wisdom of Jesus in the 21st Century

Book Design by Transcendent Publishing
www.transcendentpublishing.com

Printed in the United States of America

ISBN: 978-1-7374553-1-8

ACKNOWLEDGMENTS

I want to dedicate this book to my mother Ann, who gave me the foundation of knowing God and realizing Him in my life. It was her love of the Church and her strong faith in God, Jesus, and the Blessed Mother that shaped me as a human being. She continued to support me when I stepped away from the Church, though she strongly encouraged me to return. It was in the first thirteen years of my life, and through her influence, that created a sturdy foundation, which laid the groundwork for the evolution of my own spirituality thus far.

To my father, Horace, who passed away during the final edits of this book. I remember him saying when I was a kid, "When you die, you die, that's it, you're gone," and then he would chuckle.

I was afraid to die back then, and I believe that was his way of putting my fears to rest. But what about his fears? My father was a rock, but even rocks have hidden cracks deep within their solid mass.

After his passing, I wanted to honor Dad in a simple way, so it was perfect that I came across the following words, written by him. I call this "Empty Pockets," a gift of wisdom from a father who is gone but not forgotten…

"Death is the topic for today.
Enter with empty pockets, leave the same way.
Every day is a gift from God.

Be happy when you see the Blue sky
in the morning. That is all I have to say today."

~Horace Edward Hostetler
(July 18, 1930 – September 11, 2020)

To my husband Larry, who has been a silent support system for me through all of my endeavors over the years. It is your support on every level that has sustained me through life's revolving doorways.

To my teacher, Miss Jackie: You may no longer walk this earth with me in physical form, but your words have become my basis for understanding. You were the one who showed me the way to open the door, then gave me the space to turn the handle and walk across the threshold. Until we meet again, in this world or the next.

To my daughter Tiffany, you have always believed in me and have been my righthand woman in sharing my story. You are a true visionary, and your positivity is what will carry you forward through the rest of this lifetime.

To my grandchildren, Hazel, Mikey, Kade, Liam and Kaylani. You are the future of this World. I have faith that you will each do great things in life as you make your own mark upon this planet.

To my Council, I am so incredibly grateful for the work that has been done between us. Your loving guidance during this writing process has allowed us both to be heard. As your light shines through me, my own light shines even brighter. Over the years, you have assisted, in giving our work a platform to be seen and heard from. An equal exchange of energy has been established and a relationship solidified. To you, my dear Council, I extend a deep, heartfelt "Thank You," for without you this version of me would cease to exist.

CONTENTS

FOREWORD

Blow the Trumpet!

*"If it were not for Me,
your World would be thirsty.*

*If it were not for Me,
your World would hunger.*

*If it were not for Me, you would never know the true
meaning of The Kingdom of Heaven.*

*It is upon His Holy Chariot where I was sent to Deliver
your World from her sinful ways.*

*Be not so literal in your thinking for it Stifles
the Flow of Holy Wisdom.*

*When your people can read between the lines and into
the grey matter, it is then they will be delivered to
the Promised Land."*

Jesus

December 18, 2020

INTRODUCTION

What if I said that Jesus was only the gateway to God? What if I told you that God needed a human to represent Him here on Earth, so he sent a flesh and blood man "made in His image?" What if I told you that Jesus was that messenger, the master teacher whose mission was to awaken humanity, even as He spoke to its flaws?

As a human being, now separated from Source, I believe that Jesus came to remind us not to be separate but to be connected to that oneness. As a medium and a channel, I am able to connect with the Spirit World and bring forth prophetic information, as well as the teachings, wisdom and knowledge of Jesus and other Ascended Masters.

I was baptized and raised as a Catholic. What I learned in those early days would become the foundation of my spiritual enlightenment, the space from which I was able to move on towards something bigger. This is where I found a resonance, a calling to work within the flow of something that occurred naturally within me. It was not until many years later that I discovered a name for this resonance; it is called the Tao. This is the place where I have found the spiritual evolution of my own soul's light – a platform that is fully supportive of who I am now.

I am not a guru; I am just a woman who shares her light with each of you. My life purpose is to help amplify the light within others so that they too can stand in the truth of who they are.

It is from this place of understanding that they become the teacher, passing on what they have learned to others. One gives, another receives – these are the Universal Laws in action.

In my humble opinion, there has never been a more significant time in our history to share with and remind the World of the teachings of Christ. It is the reason I was called to write this book. It in no way revolves around religious dogma, but rather embraces what I learned, particularly in childhood, about Jesus and how His teachings reach beyond the religious factions to speak to the hearts of all people.

Like all of you, I can see how the world is changing around us, seemingly at a frenetic pace. While these changes can certainly be jarring, it is through them that the masks of mankind and the political elites are being stripped away. For far too long these elites, with their insatiable lust for power, have used government to keep their proverbial thumbs on the rest of us. They try to strip away our faith in Source, so we have to depend on them for all we need. Now, however, the common man is finally awakening to the truth of who they really are.

It brings my thoughts back to the time of Christ, the days when that precious child was born in a manger. Wisemen gathered from near and far as they followed the Star of Bethlehem. Upon finding this child the wisemen left gifts of gold, frankincense, and myrrh at His feet. He was referred to as the King of Kings and was named Jesus, which holds the meaning of "God within Us."

I sense the energy under which Jesus was born is upon us once again. It reminds me of what I learned in the scriptures of His second coming. Could this be the awakening that each of us are feeling? Could this be why the lust for power, greed, and control are front and center in governments across the world? As they say, only time will tell.

I have been channeling messages from the Spirit World since 1993 and have been guided by Spirit to share some of these messages from 2013 to the present. That is what you will find in this book. These messages come from Jesus the Christ, other Ascended Masters, my own Council, and many others from the Spirit World who work with me daily. Layered within these inspired writings are directly channeled messages – these I have put in ***bold italics*** – as well as personal stories about my own life and how my faith has carried me forward through trying times. There is a flow to it, with each page holding individual wisdom for the seeking soul. I invite you to join me on this journey and together we will navigate the challenges of the world we now find ourselves in, and cultivate the wisdom to see beyond the darkness. As you move through it, I ask only that you read with an open heart, take what resonates deeply, and leave the rest behind.

> ***"You see Dear Ones, you each have a place where an understanding resides deep within you, where the truth of your own understanding is revealed to you, as it Resonates, Activates, and Awakens that internal truth from within you."***

This is the place from which this book springs. It is like the Tao – beautiful, channeled information offered for consumption and digested by each person differently so they can gain from it individually. And, just as with the Tao, when we read the passages, we are gifted with an opportunity to dig deep and tap into our own place of understanding.

In this way it becomes a guide for creating a sacred space within you, where your spirit can be fed, and your soul can become more fully awakened.

About the Channeled Messages

When I channel, there are different entities that work with and through me. They do not speak quite like you or I do; they seem to use words in a unique way, which may take a little getting used to. As you read the pages of this book, I ask you to be mindful of this fact so you can enjoy the messages in their original, authentic form.

As you will see, I often reference a particular spirit person like Jesus or Mary Magdalene; or I will mention inspired writing, which is a collaboration of sorts. I will also talk about my Council, or group of beings I work with. The Council is a collective consciousness made up of distinct energetic impressions. This *"energetic signature,"* so to speak, is how I know who I am working with as they step forth and present themselves to me at a given time.

That said, I know them only as this energy, not with individual names, though they do refer to themselves as "The Council of Nine." I once asked them why that was, and they replied simply:

"Our name is unimportant...

It is our energy that you should become familiar with. This is how we will communicate with you, from an energetic standpoint."

Now, when channeling Jesus, I can tell you the energy is quite different. He is always at my left side and presents Himself in a way that is unique and recognizable to me. He likes to speak in parables, often about love and "The Way." He connects to that Source energy of my own understanding, the energy of God.

Mary Magdalene is similar to Jesus, but her energy is feminine, and she is more direct in her communications with me. It is as if she is shouting from the rafters for us to hear the word of the Lord.

The Blessed Mother's energy is pure love – maternal, nurturing, and ever so gentle. Her messages are most often about the suffering of the world, and she speaks about the importance of prayer on a Universal level. She always connects on a heart level for me. My visions and prophetic impressions from Our Lady began in the early 1990s.

St. Theresa is another spirit person I have channeled. Her energy is warm, loving, vibrant, and full of deep wisdom. I can feel her presence so strongly, it is like she is standing before me in the flesh.

Saint Germaine has a warmth to him. He presents himself on a wave of healing energy, a wave of purple light which then becomes the Violet Flame. He communicates information about how to assist those in the healing of themselves. He will teach you that by burning away what no longer serves you individually, he can and will assist the collective conscious-ness of our planet.

The Inspired Messages

When I do inspired writing, I allow the flow of my Council or any of the other entities who work with me to come through, as if I am hearing a whisper in my ear. I am present in the experience and allow the wisdom of my soul to lead the way, though there are moments when those entities briefly take over. This is when they layer channeled pieces of information into the messages that are written. It is a collaboration of sorts, the space where two worlds – spirit and human —collide and become one.

The Best Way to Read This Book

As mentioned, this book was written in the way of the Tao – with flow and purpose, one page moving onto the next, speaking to each individual, yet universal in nature. I encourage you to sit with it as if visiting an old friend. Allow each page to tell you its own story so that you can absorb the wisdom before you. Allow your own soul to bubble to the surface. Remember, emotions connect us to our feelings, and it is our feelings that connect us to our truth. Enjoy the journey!

THE BUDDING MEDIUM

A Visitation from a Grandmother in Spirit

From my earliest memory, I was imbued with the notion of God, or *Source*, and had a strong connection with Him. To this day, God has been a major influence in my life, and it is by His hand that I am led.

I was, after all, raised by an Italian Catholic mother, and this is where my connection to God became solidified. My mom always had a rosary within reach, and she taught me how to believe in the power of prayer.

I learned from an early age how to live by the Ten Commandments, and I always reflected upon what was a sin and what was not. As a young girl, I tried ever so hard to abide by the rules and confessed when I thought that any sin would cast me to hell. Oh, how different life appears when seen through the eyes of a child!

By the age of eight, my spirituality already had a solid foundation, one built upon the teachings of the Church. As part of those teachings, I had been told there were no such things as ghosts, and that the dead lived in heaven. Then something was revealed to me – something that was not spoken about in the church or in the home that I was raised in – that would change my life in a very profound way.

My mom's mother's name was Louise Pulio. She passed away in 1967, when I was about two and a half years old, so I never really knew her. However, as I have learned along the way, those in the Spirit World sure do know us!

It was a typical day at our house and bedtime came quickly. I shared a room with my sister Tina, and I was not a fan of the dark. It was on a warm summer's evening in late August when my grandmother stopped by for a visit. She appeared in my bedroom in the strangest way.

At that age, my sleep was usually sound and uninterrupted, according to my mother. Yet on this one particular evening I was awakened by a blue electric light that filled the room. As I looked around, I could see clearly through this indigo-colored light, and every tangible thing in my room was crystal clear.

It was what I saw in the next moment that took my breath away. There, before me was a coffin, but not like any you would see in a funeral home today. It was very plain and had the shape of the coffins from Dracula films. The outside edges were lit with a very bright white light. The rest of the coffin was the same electric blue as the light that lit up my bedroom.

As I gazed upon the coffin, the lid slid open to reveal someone inside, a woman I immediately recognized as my mom's mother. My grandmother smiled softly at me, and as I sat straight up in my bed, she did the same in her coffin. What happened next is as vivid today as it was that night so long ago.

As I sat frozen in my bed, Grandmother Pulio opened her arms and stretched them out towards me. Then, out of nowhere, seven white crosses came from her heart and flew directly into my own. I could feel each cross, one by one, enter into my body. It happened quickly, at the speed of light, yet at the same time it felt like the scene was unfolding in slow motion.

I screamed out, sure that I was going to die right then and there. I thought that she was going to take me away and that I was going to burn in hell for some sinful thing I must have done. Mind you, my sister never woke up during this whole experience, which to this day I still do not understand.

Next thing I knew, I had hustled it out of my bedroom and into my mother's room. She told me it was just a dream and to go back to bed. I thought, *Go back to bed in that room? No way!*

We never spoke about this so-called dream again. Of course, I knew it had not been a dream at all, but a visitation. I also realized that there was something quite different about me. Back then, I was frightened by what happened on that warm August night. Today, I see it as a gift – the moment I was opened to a life of purpose and given a glimpse of what and who I was to become.

To this day, my purpose is still unfolding in the most amazing ways as I continue to embrace the spiritual side of my life's work.

"As you move forward and into this book of record know that it is by the Divine Hand of God that this Author, this Woman, this Spiritual Teacher gives thanks.

She not only gives thanks to God, but she also thanks the masters who are in spirit. Those who have entrusted her with sharing their messages and inspiration as a way to bring peace to this ever-changing World."
The Council of Nine

Author's Reflections

I share this story to introduce myself to you, so that you can get a feel for how the Spirit World has chosen to work with me. You may be asking yourself, who is this woman who found it so important to write this book? I can tell you that the passion for the words written within these pages burned from deep within me.

I was told by my Council that I needed to put some of the information channeled throughout the years in book form, and I did so without question. "It is time," they said, and that was all I needed to hear.

It is with great joy that I share with all of you what God has gifted to me. I hope that you enjoy this living breathing testament as you allow the words before you to guide you in your own journey of self-discovery.

JESUS

Before I move into the body of this work, I wanted to share a visitation that I had with Jesus, in a dream, on April 5, 1999. I believe this was just the beginning of what was to be shared with me later on, and what I have been guided to share with each of you here. It was where the doorway was opened, an invitation sent, a stage set, an awareness documented.

"Last night, I dreamt of Christ. I saw Him; He visited me. The vision of Him began at His feet; they were bare, and the light moved upwards from there. He had on a white robe with a red cross in the center of it. His arms were opened, stretched outwards and reaching upwards. He was speaking to me; He gave me a message which I could not remember upon my awakening. There was a golden light which encompassed Christ. As I sit and write about this visitation, I feel peaceful and calm."

As I reflect upon this passage – which, by the way, was discovered "by accident" before I published this book – I cannot help but think there are no such things as coincidences. I can now see, all these years later, the meaning of what this dream, this visitation, has to offer to me now.

Seeing Jesus stand before me, beginning with His feet, shows me the connection that I have with the world I am living in now: very grounded in my human experience yet connected to my faith.

His arms opened, stretched out to me in an upwards fashion, brings me back to my grandmother's visitation as a young girl. The seven white crosses coming from her heart and landing within my own, were in preparation of things to come. An awareness piqued of how I was already tuned into my gift of mediumship, and the occasional prophetic information given.

His white robe connects me to the possibility of all things, the purity of Spirit, the resurrection as promised. The red cross is symbolic of the blood of Christ, and of those who are willing to place the cloak of humility upon their own shoulders. The golden-colored aura is the pathway towards enlightenment.

It brings my awareness to those who came before me and have witnessed what I have – for example, painters like Giovanni Battista Piazzetta,[1] with his *Madonna and Child appearing to St. Philip Neri,* and Titian, who is best known for *St. John the Evangelist on Patmos.*[2] These and other artists throughout the centuries have used their craft to share their experiences of this golden aura. Today, their incredible and inspiring works hang in the museums around the world, a testament to Christ's presence in our lives.

In that dream, Jesus was speaking to me, preparing me for direct communication so I could become the scribe for His messages.

These are just my own experiences, to be consumed by you, the reader, in an individual fashion. There are no judgments, just love… No hate, just peace…No limits or boundaries, just freedom of expression.

Author's Reflections

This is a great place to stop for a moment and tap into that beautiful spirit of your own. Tune into the voice of your own soul's wisdom and allow it to remind you of who you are and who you were meant to be.

See where the God of your own understanding has risen from within – guiding you, teaching you, showing you, leading you towards your purposeful moments in life.

It is from here you can validate those moments and allow them to be displayed from your human perspective.

---

[1] Piazetta, Giovanni Battista. *Madonna and Child appearing to St. Philip Neri.* (1725). https://www.nga.gov/collection/art-object-page.46181.html
[2] Titian. St. John the Evangelist on Patmos. (1553/1555). https://www.nga.gov/collection/art-object-page.43725.html

I want to start with the following channeled message, one of the first from Jesus The Christ that began to flow freely through me. I was always connected to Him through my upbringing in the Church, but as they say, the Spirit World will use those who can communicate what will best serve the sitter. In this case the sitter is you, the reader, so please enjoy the journey.

JESUS'S UNIVERSAL WISDOM

Okay, everyone, this was a big one and unexpected, even by me. It speaks volumes on having faith and trust.

"Blessed are those who believe, for healed they shall be. Rejoice one and all, for He resides within your hearts. Access Him there, and you too shall know your truth.

Give unto Him your sorrows, your pain, and He will fill you with love and with light. Your heart will become joyful, and your soul will shine.

Be not afraid, for you are never alone. Even in your darkest moments He holds your hand. Believe in Me and so you to shall believe in Him.

The Lord God is your savior, and all things are possible through Him. It is faith in the unseen and trust in the unknown that lights your way.

Be not afraid to step from the shadows and into the light, for your greatest gifts lie there. Go forth, seek, and so ye shall find."

Channeled message from Jesus, April 11, 2013

Author's Reflections

As I read these words and allow them to permeate my being, I am reminded of the many paths that lay before the masses to walk upon.

The pathways are different, and for each of us, an individual journey. The answers to a spiritual calling from deep within will guide us forth. Some people are guided toward religious dogma, others by spiritual gurus, but all paths will lead you to the God of your own understanding.

It is time for the spiritual revolution to pour from this earth, as we stand without fear cloaked in our own faith. This is where we can each connect to the spiritual forces that have guided us throughout this lifetime.

Jesus taught us about the way. In the end, it is up to you to decide what the way means for you. Only you can decide how to travel towards the oneness that will absorb you into its love and grace. Only you can decide what and who God is for you.

Take a moment and reflect on the words written. This is where you can allow the truth to rise from within you and validate His existence.

MY FATHER'S HOUSE

The Omega Institute in Rhinebeck, New York is a camp where spiritualists go to study with teachers from all over the world. It is there that I have had some of the most amazing experiences in my spiritual journey, each one serving me in the form of enlightenment for the good of my soul's evolution. Each trip to Omega has been a blessing, but my reflections now bring me to the summer of 2013.

During one experience while there, I was visited by Jesus, and I remember His essence and vibration so clearly. As He appeared before me, I asked Him, *Why are you here*? He said to me:

"Because you asked Me to be."

As I sat with Him, He asked me to travel with Him and told me,

"I have something of value to show you."

He then took me on a journey, and He showed me the true meaning of,

"In my Father's house are many mansions"

Jesus explained it to me as a representation of the levels of our soul's growth and how we all fit into this puzzle called life. He then shared with me these words:

"You are each on different levels for growth, unique and individual to your soul's needs."

He showed me that when we do return to spirit we will continue to work on that same level. This is where, according to Jesus, our soul moves onto after living an earthly life. He then said to me:

"You are always striving for growth in whatever plane your soul resides."

During our time together I could clearly see a mansion, and this mansion consisted of many different floors, all vibrating to different colors. I could see multiple people working on each level of awareness as they peacefully went about the work at hand.

Jesus made me aware of how many of us will walk a similar path when we are alive in this world. His next words to me were these:

"Each of you are here to teach one another from the perspective of your own life experiences."

He spoke to me about how this was where we can learn from one another if we are truly open to that particular lesson. This place I visited was filled with love and light. There were teachers, or guides, working with each individual soul. These souls were working towards perfection as a way to reach the next floor. Jesus then told me this:

"Each floor is just a steppingstone towards that perfect oneness that you are each seeking with God."

When I returned and before Jesus left me, He asked me to do something for Him.

"Tell all of the people in this room, those who will listen to you about what you have been shown. Tell them how they are each individual lights who strive for the same thing, oneness with Source, with God."

I was reminded during my time with Jesus that in the grand scheme of things, we are all light. We all come from love, and this incarnation is just another avenue from which to learn. This is the place where we will continue to grow on a soul level, for now, as we each seek enlightenment. I was able to see how each individual soul, each person, has teachers in the Spirit World called guides. It is my guides who assure me that when a person is ready, their guides will step forth and make their presence known in order to assist each person in their spiritual journey.

Channeled from Jesus, August 20, 2013

Author's Reflections

During the time of this workshop, I was being taught by two spiritual tutors — one American and one English. Both of these men are well-known in the spiritual community and to be taught by them was exciting, to say the least.

*Now, during my drive to New York from Illinois, I was told that something magical would happen for me during my time there. It was what I needed to hear. While on the road, I seemed to have been placed in some scary situations and being alone had become stressful. There were even a handful of times when I wanted to turn around and go home. Yet I was encouraged by my Council to continue on. "**Stay the course**," they said, which of course I did. I was looking forward to seeing what would transpire when I immersed myself in this spiritual experience.*

I was shown that indeed, it would be an eye-opening week, and one that I shall never forget.

The visitation with Jesus you just read about happened to transpire on our first day in workshop, and as you can imagine I was extremely excited by it. My bubble, however, was soon to be popped by the American tutor. As I saw it, his ego was a bit inflated, and he seemed to want people to believe that only he was gifted enough to communicate with the ascended masters. He had a group of followers who came along with him and hung on his every word.

The place where Jesus had told me to stand up and relay His message to everyone who would listen pulled at me. I of course had told Jesus, "No way am I sharing this," and I sat unmoved.

After numerous people had shared, that Jesus had come to them, the American tutor asked, "Is there anyone else who Jesus has shown up for?"

Out of nowhere my hand went into the air. I was still thinking, no way, while asking myself what is happening here? I found myself standing before the group with the microphone in my hand.

I proceeded to tell everyone what Jesus had said to me and what I had seen. All eyes were on me, and I could feel that the people in this classroom were resonating with what I had to say. The American tutor then came to the edge of the stage and looked at me, his eyes going up and down my body. What he said next shocked me.

"Do you actually think that Jesus has the time to show up for someone like you?" As I sat down, completely mortified, the tutor told me that I had conjured Jesus up in my mind and that my own imagination had me believing He was speaking with me. The experience I described was impossible he said, then he moved on, leaving me feeling deflated. The rest of the day I kept quiet and to myself. I began to doubt in the guidance from my Council and was confused as to why I had really been guided to be there. The rest of this week would have many twists and turns, which I will share as we move into the next experience.

The magic is worth the read!

I share this reflection here to tell you that no person, no matter how famous they are, can ever declare what he does not know. We are each tested throughout our lives. It is how we choose to study for and pass the test that matters most.

Jesus told his followers, "What I can do so can you and more." Now it is up to you to choose how you share your message with those who may or may not be ready to hear it. Yes, the validation when one accepts those messages is wonderful, but we can also learn much about ourselves from rejection, especially when it comes from those who we look to as our teachers. This is where we will see our inner strength rise, as we validate our own truth, no matter what someone else tells us to believe about ourselves.

Today I ask you to believe in what you think is impossible. This is where you can begin to listen closely to what some have called "the voices within their own minds."

THE BOOK OF WISDOM

Jesus would again make His presence known while I was in that classroom at Omega. The instructor had just led us into a deep state of meditation called "the power." This is the place where we put our human ego aside and commune with Spirit. My teacher Miss Jackie would call this "going direct."

As I sat in the power, I could feel Jesus' approach. He sat beside of me, and He handed me a book of wisdom. A page was bookmarked, and when I opened the book to that page, the word I saw and read was "Hope."

Then Jesus spoke to me.

"Hope, teach people about hope and continue to remind them about My Father's mansion and His many rooms."

He showed me visions of all of the learning we do on the other side when we are still in spirit form. He showed me how hope connects us to faith, and where both can be accessed, saying that,

"One is the doorway and the other the threshold."

Jesus went on to say,

"The flow, the light, will naturally occur for all. Hope is the intent needed and that which leads you towards faith. Faith is the unbreakable bond you have with truth. Access it through hope, and so it shall be."

Jesus taught me that this is how we humans can reconnect to the pathway which leads us towards that oneness with God. That is, after all, what it is all about. As we have fallen away from our authentic self in spirit form, we have taken on a human body that cloaks our light. This is why the guidance given is so important, as it helps us to access what we have temporarily forgotten.

Channeled from Jesus August 20, 2013

Author's Reflections

The above visitation, which happened on the second day of my weeklong retreat, was clearly a powerful one. But it was what happened as the workshop opened that day that set the stage for understanding my week of miracles.

The workshop always opened with a meditation by one of the tutors. On this day, the American tutor took to the platform and said, "Have I got something special to share with you this morning."

He went on to tell the class that Jesus had come to him as he prepared his teaching syllabus for the day. He then said Jesus had given him an incredibly special meditation that he had to share with us.

For the next few minutes, I listened in shock as this American Tutor spoke. He stated that, "Jesus showed me His father's mansion and the different levels of awareness. All of the colors that go with the different levels of awakening are here and it is where we go when we cross over." He then added rather gleefully, "Would you like me to take you there?" The class of course was over the moon, while I sat there, pretty darn mad and wondering just when the magic of this week was going to begin. The tutor, whom I had looked up to and respected, had taken what Jesus said to me and claimed it as his own message, as if the previous day had never happened!

Jesus showing up and giving me nuggets of wisdom was magic in and of itself, but I felt that something was missing. I again questioned why I had made this trip in the first place.

Looking back, my hope was a bit squashed, and my faith depleted because my own ego would not allow me to see what was happening. We

THE BOOK OF WISDOM

have all been there, where someone may have made us feel less-than and we believed it. In fact, I would say this is a great time for you to stop for a moment and reflect on areas of your own life when something similar may have happened to you. How were you able to overcome it? You never know who you may be able to help through your personal experiences.

Read on for the next miraculous experience that my Council had in store for me.

ST. THERESA'S WISDOM ON LOVE...

One of the reasons I had gone to Omega in 2013 was to further develop my Trance Mediumship abilities. Trance is an altered state in which the medium allows the spirit people to briefly use their bodies and their voices. In other words, the medium allows themselves to become the vessel, free from the interference of their own mind, through which the spirit people can be seen and heard from in this world. This is an energy exchange; a sacred communication called the "blending" of minds. This form of mediumship requires the medium to surrender, and it takes years of practice and dedication, however, those who become seasoned in their craft can offer people in the séance room a truly sacred experience.

The message I am about to share with you was channeled through me on day three of the workshop, and it has stuck with me ever since.

It is a powerful yet loving message that speaks to each of our own hearts in one way or another. It carries within it the energy of the Christ and what He came to teach the World.

In my humble opinion, this should become the core of our own teaching, the standard that each of us adheres to as we raise our families or just move through our own lives.

Please know that wisdom appears in all forms. The wisdom that is layered within St. Theresa's words are some of the most powerful that I have ever read.

"Please be mindful of this, that what you teach to your own children today, will become the foundation on which they will teach their own in the future.

Plant the seeds of love within their hearts now, and they will surely know peace for a lifetime.

It is through your own understanding where you must apply these principles.

It is from here, and where each child must be given order and discipline to learn from, yet it must be built upon a foundation of love.

For if it is not built upon love, then that foundation will surly crumble beneath their feet."

Channeled message from St. Theresa, August 22, 2013

Author's Reflections

As I reflect on the day, I can tune into the energy that I had decided to dwell in during that time. This particular message came through while we were sitting in the power. People were asked to share what had come to them and from whom.

This was when I said, "No way! I will not share my experiences only to be scolded once again."

We only had a half-day in workshop that day because there would be a trance demonstration in the evening. The tutors said they needed the rest, so we were left with the afternoon to do as we wanted.

At lunchtime, I found myself sitting alone. As I ate, I said to my Council and to God, "Why have you brought me here? You told me that something magical would happen. By the time this evening comes, you better show me why I am here, or I am going home!"

All I can say is, when you ask, be prepared to receive.

That evening I arrived early for the demonstration because I wanted a front row seat and some time to reflect in the space. There happened to be another student there and he was watching a woman set up the stage area. When I asked what was going to happen, the woman said that the English tutor was going to go into trance, and someone from the audience would be picked to sit in the chair before him. The American tutor, she added, would be picking the person.

One lucky person would be one-on-one with the trance medium and receive a message from the entity he was channeling. Before I knew it, I was declaring out loud, in front of these two people, that I was going to get picked. I said, "Do you hear me God, I need you to put me in that chair!"

Soon people began to pour in until the room was filled with more than two hundred. I did indeed get what I thought was a front row seat, only to be shocked when the followers of the American tutor sat down in front of me and the other people in my row. Incensed, I said to one of my classmates, "Isn't this something? He is setting it up so that one of his own gets picked." Then a woman from our class came out of nowhere with a chair in hand. She placed it right next to me, blocking the aisle before the demonstration began. The American tutor ended up standing in that aisle, unaware that the dynamics had changed. It wasn't until it was time to choose an audience member that he realized he could not pass by.

We all had our hands in the air, hoping to be picked. He stood for what felt like an eternity, then I felt a hand around my wrist. I was being pulled from my chair! It was me; I was picked to sit before the English tutor as he sat in trance. What happened next would change my life forever.

Yes, miracles do happen, and what the channeled entity spoke to me about was my purpose and how my voice was key to fulfilling that purpose. He told me who I was, and what I had incarnated into this lifetime to do. He told me many things that I do not wish to share at this time, but I want you to know that I have tried to honor my purpose through the work that I do.

I left that séance room feeling lifted like never before; I also felt the eyes of many people on me. The next day in class, everyone wanted to talk to and work with me. What a stark contrast from day one! Not everyone was pleasant, however. One of the American tutor's students actually came over to me and stated in front of other classmates, that I did not deserve to be picked because that seat was promised to her! It was another arrow shot in my direction, but the messages received during my first three days and on that particular evening had taught me how to overcome.

That was a part of the gift for me, part of the magic promised to me. This was when I discovered that I had even more confidence to share the words of Jesus from a platform, supported by my own words and spoken in my own voice. This book of record becomes the fulfillment of my purpose!

Today is a great day to find your own voice and to honor what pours from you. Purpose comes in many forms; find your own purpose and you will find fulfilment in your journey.

THE VIOLET FLAME OF ST. GERMAINE

"That pure violet light that pours into your being, supports your spiritual health and is the color associated with your spiritual path.

It supports you as you walk this journey and is always available to you. Once called upon, its influence is undeniable.

This violet light helps to elevate your spirit and is the color that we associate with your spiritual beliefs. When the path is made clear to you, call upon this violet flame to light your way so that you may never get lost upon your journey home."

~Saint Germaine

I find this beautiful shade of color to be more than that for me, as it connects me with the energy of healing as well. St. Germaine's violet flame helps to sweep away your fears, worries, sorrows, and burdens. It helps to clear the way so that your heart may be healed, and your soul elevated.

When you connect to this violet light, you open yourselves up to a connection of higher wisdom and guidance. Our spiritual teachers here on earth such as priests, pastors and spiritual leaders will adorn themselves in this purple color. It helps to elevate them spiritually and assists them as they heal the world through prayer and the written word.

Channeled and Inspired Writing September 11, 2013

Author's Reflections

If you can quiet your minds, even for five minutes, you can then allow the quiet to be filled with the color purple. It is a great way to begin to heal all aspects of your lives.

I like to sit with my eyes closed and just begin breathing, allowing each breath in to become an open portal for this light. As I exhale, I let go of any dense energy that needs to be released. This is how I make space for that purple light to replace what is not serving me now.

The Violet Flame needs only your invitation to activate the healing within you. So, breathe deep, use daily, and enjoy the journey.

JESUS ON HOW WE CAN FEED THE WORLD...

In the bible story known as the miracle of five loaves and two fishes, Jesus stood before a crowd of thousands and preached. The crowd grew hungry and demanded to be fed. The disciples grew worried and asked,

Master, how will we feed so many when we have not enough?

Jesus calmly blessed the food that they had, then asked His disciples to distribute the food among the people. After everyone had eaten, it was told that twelve baskets of food remained. Jesus provided the people on that day with the miracle of endless fish and bread. He called upon God and used the Universe to provide and not one person went hungry on that day.

What Jesus did was show the people that if you desire something, just ask and it will be provided. He showed His followers the power behind their own thoughts. Jesus demonstrated how to manifest what the people had asked for, without worry.

How did He do it?

He was able to achieve it because he knew, without question, that it was possible. He had no doubts or fears blocking His way, and His belief in His actions had made it a reality.

Jesus taught us...

"What I can do so can you and more. You too can create and draw to you anything you desire as long as you believe in it."

Jesus knew the power of the Law of Attraction and the lesson taught on this day. In the words of Spirit...

"Let not fear nor doubt create a roadblock to your dreams and desires."

Inspired and Channeled by Jesus on October 29, 2013

Author's Reflections

When it comes to manifesting things within our lives there are many tools for us to use. The one thing we seem to forget is to trust in the process. We allow doubt and fear to act as roadblocks because we are out of alignment with the true power of manifestation.

A great way to look at manifesting anything is like this.

The Mind becomes the Roadmap.

The Heart becomes the Vehicle.

Your Feelings become the Fuel.

Follow the route set, make sure your vehicle is in good working order and gas up that car. You will be sure to make it to where it is you desire to be as long as you do not stray from the path. Your destination has everything to do with getting what you want as long as you allow the GPS system in the vehicle to guide you there.

If you can be in perfect alignment and release your order (control) without fear or doubt, you will multiply your blessings tenfold.

Ask, Believe, Release, and Receive!!!

JUST BELIEVE

Faith is believing in something that we cannot see with our physical eyes, we cannot touch with our physical hands, and something that we cannot alter in the physical world.

Faith connects us to that higher power, whoever that may be for you. For me, that faith resides with God.

Faith is what gets us through our darkest moments, as faith assures us that our voices and our prayers are being heard.

Faith is validated in our beliefs, and where we can watch the miracles unfold within our own lives daily.

Having faith is like breathing. None of us focus on every breath, but breath is what sustains our physical existence.

Faith is not something that you can buy from the store, it is a gift that we all carry within us.

Faith is the gift that connects us to God, and when in doubt just allow faith to carry you through.

Inspired Writing, November 14, 2013

Author's Reflections

As I reflect on the word faith, I can see how some people might need a tangible object to make it real. This is where they fall from the path of belief because they did not trust that the breadcrumbs that were laid out before them would lead them home.

Jesus taught me that to get a good handle on faith we can use hope to connect the dots. Hoping is good, and when your hopes become solid, your beliefs back it up. When your beliefs become solid, you can grab onto faith's hand and allow it to be the final piece of the puzzle.

Though hope is also invisible, for some it provides an easier path toward understanding the invisible strength that the faithful rely on.

Faith is inside of you; all you have to do is believe.

LET'S TALK ABOUT GOD

Everyone has a different way that they worship God in their lives. We also have our own perception of what God may look like. But one thing is for certain, and that's God's love for every soul on this planet.

Now, I talk about God today because I want to honor the source of every living thing. I am aware of God's grace, and it is through Him that I am blessed in many ways.

As I write this, I understand that there may be some of you who might question God's existence. I am here to tell you that it is okay for you to do so. I realize that each person will come to find the definition of what they call or see God to be, when the timing is right for them. This is called recognizing the God of your own understanding.

When I am fortunate enough to sit with those who question God, I just refer to God as the light inside of them. I do not judge their beliefs, nor do I try to change their point of view.

I know that when they are ready, they too will understand His glory. I am of the belief that everyone has had that profound moment in their life when a prayer has been answered. This is when they give thanks to that invisible force behind the blessing.

For today, I ask that you recognize your many blessings, and give thanks to the God of your own understanding, as you recognize and feel His profound Love for you.

Inspired writing, November 26, 2013

Author's Reflections

Anyone who knows me knows that I am a person of faith and have a deep belief in God. I understand that each person's knowledge of God is distinct, just as you and I are distinct from one another. That is what makes us unique in our lives and in our own beliefs. That is why we gravitate towards people who are of the same energy as us.

No matter where you are when it comes to your belief in God, no one can judge you for it. In your own timing and in this world or the next, your answer to His existence will be made clear as love lights the way.

ONE GOD, ONE SOURCE OF LIGHT

*"You are all connected, each of you are, as you are all
fed from the same Source, the same Light."*

Today I glimpsed the beauty of all religions, and I witnessed the
way that they each worship the God of their understanding. I
then became a witness to the single stream of light that
sustained them all.

*In this beautiful courtyard the faithful gathered, each using the tools
of their religion to connect them with the Divine. As I watched, they were
all filled with the same light of God's love. Even though they all had a
different view of how God may look, a different way of worshiping Him,
there was only one stream of light that filled them all.*

The most beautiful part of this vision is how we are all connected.

*"It is in this single stream of light that you are each
given all that you have need of. From your strength to
your faith, it is from this single stream of light
that you are each nourished."*

The only difference between you and I, is how we have chosen to
worship God. The connection for each of us is the same, for He
knows our hearts and supports our paths.

I encourage you to experience and be opened to all forms of
religious beliefs and practices without judgment. I ask that you too,
can find acceptance, because in the end, it is through this single
stream of light that your humanness will be fed, and your own soul
awakened.

Vision written and Channeled on January 10, 2014

Author's Reflections

We are all created from a single source of light, this is true. Yet this source has given us the gift of free will, which offers us discernment to navigate a spiritual path towards Him. How we choose to do this is up to us, and it is through each path discovered that we learn new ways towards Him. This is a great time to sit and validate your own path towards the God of your own understanding. Tap into that feel-good part of your own ritual and see how you may be able to shine a light on that path for another, who may also be seeking.

THE BLOOD MOON
DURING HOLY WEEK

I want to share with you the experience of seeing the magnificent moon turn from white to blood-red. I would like to impress upon you how profound it was for this rare event – a total lunar eclipse of the moon – to happen during our Holy Week. It was both symbolic and magical all at the same time.

My feelings were anxious throughout the day as I knew I needed to bear witness to this event. I was like a child waiting for the magic of Santa Claus to visit me on Christmas Eve. I was not quite sure why until I laid my eyes upon the full moon.

I was jolted out of my sleep at 1:30 a.m., and as I looked out of the window there she was – half-red, half-white. I was not only imbued with excitement, I was also brought to the emotion and feeling of the sorrowful mysteries that we pray on the rosary. This rare celestial occasion delivered me to the Crucifixion of Christ, and this is when I began to understand.

To me, this blood moon was very symbolic of how Christ was scourged, beaten, bloodied, and battered, as His life had both purpose and meaning. This is where Jesus fulfilled the prophecy that was promised for the good of mankind.

As Pontius Pilate handed Him over to be crucified, Jesus carried the cross wearing a crown of thorns. As He struggled to walk, He was stoned by some and loved by others. As the moon continued to go from white to red, this became evident to me, and was symbolic of His suffering for us.

It made me fully aware that we are coming into a new time here on earth, an awakening of sorts, as we are blessed with new things to come. But not all of the people have recognized or can understand this truth at this time. Just like the people who stoned Christ while He carried the cross to Golgotha, they did not understand the gift that He was about to deliver to them through His suffering and eventual death.

As Jesus walked, He continued to pray for their souls. Even as His physical strength drained, His faith remained strong. He knew the purpose of His soul's work as He waited to return home. As He was nailed to the cross Jesus suffered greatly, yet He never lost His faith. This was when God's love eased Him into His last breath.

As I continued to watch the full moon change from blood red to darkness, I saw it as a parallel and very symbolic of this moment in history.

Atop the hill in Golgotha where Jesus was crucified, the sky went dark, and the earth shook below the people's feet. The non-believers panicked and ran, and I could feel their fear in that cold morning air. They were so terrified in that moment that I, standing beneath the still of that darkened sky more than two thousand years later, could physically feel it. It symbolized not only his suffering for us, but our own salvation through His sacrifice and God's love for each of us. Jesus knew that the only way to bring the awareness of the Kingdom of Heaven on Earth was to fulfill His destiny. It was through the resurrection where He demonstrated eternal life, the promise of God, delivered on the cross.

His ascension was near, and as the moon returned to her natural state of lightness, eternal life was the gift given through His crucifixion.

So, for today, I ask you to remember the sacrifice that was made on your behalf by Christ and know that His love for you is everlasting.

Inspired and Written on April 15, 2014

THE BLOOD MOON DURING HOLY WEEK

Author's Reflections

This long-ago writing brings me to the subject of astrology, and what was going on in the heavens the night of the Blood Moon. I believe it played a huge part in what I felt and saw. The planets were in alignment with days of the past; the moon was guiding our way and lending its light to us here on earth.

Astrology has a lot to do with how we think and feel; planets even dictate our actions. Just as the timetable was laid out in the writing above, astrology can do the same for each of us individually.

Astrologically speaking, numbers do not lie. Each person's Astrological path is laid out numerically by the degree their birth planets are aligned within the heavens above. This is one of the best roadmaps to help us understand our individual personalities, purpose, and paths in life.

I would like to encourage each of you to go see an astrologer and have your stars mapped out in real time. This will give you a clear picture of what was, what is, and what is to come your way.

THE LAMB OF GOD IS UPON YOU

"*When I die, I will be more alive than I am right now, you may be able to take away my body, but you can never touch my soul.*"

These are the words of John the Baptist. He was a teacher, and his platform was through baptism.

"*It is through the water where I am cleansed.*"

As he invited those to step forth, he said:

"*The way is near, and it is through baptism where your sins are washed away.*" Look no further, for God is within you, there is one to come that will speak to you the truth, and it is through the truth that you will be shown the way.*"

John was preparing the people through the platform of baptism for the teachings of the master who was to come. He would speak to them about the truth, and how the master would show them the way beyond what he could presently teach them.

He was preparing the people for the coming of Christ.

Like John, Jesus understood that His body was just the vehicle for the messages to come through. He understood that He was a soul first, yet He was also a spiritual teacher who lived an earthly life.

He reminds all of us that our souls are everlasting, and when we die, our souls will ascend to paradise. This is where we will be reconnected fully to Source once again. He teaches us that we will carry the experiences of this lifetime with us to eternity.

This is also to remind you that your soul has a purpose, just as Jesus's did. It is through this journey we call life that this purpose is fulfilled.

You may have been raised in one religion, only to find yourself now following a different path. This has happened because there is something to be learned beyond your original belief systems. Jesus, in my own understanding, teaches us to go beyond just one modality.

As you go about your day, be grateful for every experience that you have had and know this:

"Every teacher who crosses your path, has placed a light upon the pathway. They did so as a way for you to follow it. It is through each pathway given, that will help to guide you towards your own soul's destiny."

Channeled and Inspired Writing April 18, 2014

Author's Reflections

My mind goes to this part of the message: John teaches us that we will carry the experiences of this lifetime with us throughout eternity.

It reminds me of what I have been taught over the years, that every deed we do is carried with us to heaven and reviewed. We cannot get away from it and eventually we will have to face the things we have refused to face during this incarnation.

This message is a great reminder to be good stewards of our lives. Through what is called baptism, we are forgiven our sins and in Christ we are baptized.

Make peace where peace is needed, apply forgiveness where forgiveness is warranted. Allow yourselves the gift of grace to heal the broken pieces within your own lives while you are still of flesh and blood. This way, you can begin to clear away the karma, so that in your life review, you will see how you have helped another, along with yourselves to heal.

WHEN WE WALK
WITH THE MASTERS

In the winter of 2010, I read for a man on one of my jobsites. I had a regular job just like each of you do — I spent thirty-three years as a truckdriver and heavy equipment operator until I retired in 2018. I worked this job to pay the bills while nurturing my spirituality, and I always allowed myself the opportunity to embrace both worlds at the same time. It was by choice that my light would not be hidden away because my spiritual heart was always on full display. Today I have a deep sense of gratitude for all the people who crossed my path over those years, and especially those like this man who allowed me the privilege of taking a glimpse into his past.

I wanted to share this particular story with you as it touches on the life and times of Jesus and His crucifixion. It was a past lifetime that was presented to this man on this day, a gift from Spirit to us both.

I remember it was very cold, with the temperature well below zero and a sharp, unforgiving wind. Bundled up we all were, as we watched this gentleman work diligently building a shaft from timbers. He was deliberate in his measurements; he knew that everything needed to be perfectly level. The timbers were at least thirty feet tall; they became the four corners and the stability of the shaft.

Suddenly, his past lifetime began to come into my awareness. I was taken back to the days of Christ and the Crucifixion. As I watched the man work, I saw his clothing and appearance change. This is when the vision of his job became apparent to me. The timbers began to transform themselves into the beams of the cross, and the message was clear.

When he was done, I asked if I could share the vision with him. He looked at me with a strange expression and said, "Go ahead." This is when the beauty of the vision garnered credence and I told him:

"You were a Master Carpenter, an overseer of the work and builder of the crosses during the time of Jesus's life and crucifixion." I then described to him in detail his work ethic as the Master Carpenter.

"You took great pride in your work, and you knew that each timber for the cross needed to be perfect for the occasion."

I assured him that it was just a job, the task of a lifetime past, yet his ability to understand what the cross symbolized was in his awareness at this time.

"The strengths that you bring forth into this lifetime are those of a leader and they arise from the work you had done in the past. You should have been a carpenter, that is where your true gift lies."

He shook his head in agreement and smiled at me, then asked if this was a bad thing. *"No,"* I replied, *"you just did the job that you were delegated to do, and like today, you did your job with pride. You had no feelings one way or the other towards Christ, yet you built His cross the same as you would have built the others, with precision and pride."*

He looked at me and said, "That makes me feel proud because that is how I do my job today."

I share this story as a way to help you understand something.

Past lifetimes are only shown to assist us. If you are blessed to receive a gift in the form of a past lifetime memory, embrace the message given and take from it what applies to your life right now. Such memories are due to the duplicate energy from that past lifetime, which has become fully present to re-learn from today. As I have been shown and guided to believe, we have all lived many lives. It is from those past life memories that we can gain infinite knowledge and wisdom, so long as we are open to their influence.

When I reflect on this I am fed with the knowledge of…

"Many Masters, Many Lifetimes"

and to the idea that…

"Your soul is eternal, and its journeys are endless."
Channeled and Inspired writing, May 20, 2014

Author's Reflections

Through the gift of mediumship, I am able to see, hear, and know things about a person's life. This includes the past, the present, and the future.

The past is not only connected to your past in this lifetime. It is connected to the many lifetimes that came before the you of this incarnation. It is through the memories of those lives, that you are gifted with opportunities to learn during your life now.

There are no such things as coincidences. More often than not, when a past lifetime is presented, the person will say to me, "Funny, that's where I'm drawn to now". I always say, "Is it?" This is when I can guide them to understand that the impressions are given as a gift so they can learn what they came to learn about and move on.

If you are open to the influence of past lifetimes you will understand the connections made. For those who are not, I give you this to contemplate: Déjà vu, or those moments when you feel like you have been somewhere or done something before, are actually peeks into the past. They are a connection of energy that speaks to you on a soul level, a reminder of how you are walking a path similar to one you have traveled before.

FAITH IS AN UNSEEN FORCE

*"From one dark cloud bursts a thousand rainbows, if
only you can see beyond the parameters
of the darkness."*

T his message is all about faith and seeing beyond the unseen.

*"As each of you knows, faith cannot be
seen nor touched.*

*Nor can your faith be bought in a store as it has no
tangible container to hold it within.*

*Faith is that deep belief within you that does not need a
fancy wrapper to know that it exists.*

*Your foundation in your beliefs is where faith is born of,
and once birthed, it will remain with you
for a lifetime lived.*

*It is your faith that will deliver you to unopened
doorways, and as you cross each threshold, you will
know that your faith has delivered you home."*

So, for today, have faith and say thank you to God, for it is your
own faith from which the miracles of life are born.

Channeled May 23, 2014

Author's Reflections

Faith is truth — this is the simplest way I can describe it. When we are solid in our faith, we know that the truth of our beliefs will deliver us to what our faith is connected to.

If you feel like you are lacking faith, look no further than an answered prayer. Look no further than your solid belief in something that you knew was going to come to pass. Look no further than your present moment.

Ask yourself: What has delivered me through the most difficult moments in my life? This is when you will see it was your faith in something that had been there all along.

THE POWER STRUCTURES
OF TODAY'S WORLD

*"As one-man stumbles, lost in the fog of confusion, he
comes upon another man who has remained
calm and still.*

*The confused man looks at the other man and says,
'How can you be so calm when the world
is in such turmoil?'*

*The man of great resolve looks to the confused man and
says, 'Fear is only compounded by fear and such fear
creates chaos and delusion.'*

*Feed not into this fear and it dissipates. As you release
the grip that fear has placed upon your own heart, you
will then see that it was nothing more than an illusion,
an illusion created by your thoughts.*

*Be not a follower my friend of such thinking,
and you are free."*

Spirit wants to remind you today that we are each fed the illusion of another person's thinking (the biggest sources being television and the internet). When we can become aware of this and mindful of which stories we allow into our minds and hearts, we become the arbiter of our own lives.

Yes, there are things you need to be aware of (i.e. current events), but to what extent is up to you. Fear seems to be the biggest driving force behind each cause today. It is happening because our fear is so easily tapped into and manipulated. Remembering this may bring a sense of calm into your life.

"Some things are sensationalized for ratings, political reasons, and social views. Decipher for yourself what resonates as truth, and you will see past the smoke and mirrors behind the story. Discernment is key here."

Once you are able to do this, the fear that was stirred within you calms and the layers of truth are revealed to you. This can help to heal those big world events, as you become free to apply love or prayer, where and when needed. You can even work from a hands-on perspective if you choose to.

We all have causes that are important to us; the question is to what extent do we participate in those causes?

"Let not another do your thinking for you, as you stand firmly in the truth of the causes you are fighting for."

This was written six and a half years ago, and as I put this book together in November of 2020 it holds even more truth. In fact, it goes to the heart of why I am writing it.

"In today's world fear seems to be even more powerful than ever, as the masses are lulled into a state of denial. One man pitted against another, through a manufactured truth."

This is like in the times of Christ, when the tax collectors only cared about what you owed and not about how it was hurting your human lives. If you did not pay the tax collector, then you would have to pay the piper in another form, even if it meant giving up your one and only trusted mule.

Inspired and Channeled, May 29th, 2014

Author's Reflections

My thoughts take me to the division we are feeling here in America, due largely to politics and political correctness. How did it happen? It happened because we have not discerned for ourselves whether what we are being told is absolute truth or just plain fodder.

Are we an experiment for the powerful seeking to maintain control over the masses? I would say yes, to an extent. If we pay attention to how they are doing it, we can then discern that fear is the driving force here. This is where we can begin to take our power back.

It doesn't matter if it is a virus, fear of catching it, or extremism towards those who do not share in that fear. In the end, we are all subjected to the fearmongering.

The wise man tells us not to be a follower of such thinking, and we will be free. Freedom is the gift, and it rides on the coat tails of Free Will. We do not have to be bullies in our convictions, yet we must allow others to peacefully coexist within this world of many, through the choices they deem right for themselves.

THE TEACHING OF JESUS

The teachings of Jesus are laced and intertwined throughout all religious orders in this world. There is not one that can claim Him as their own, for He was born of a purpose, and that purpose was for the salvation of mankind.

Through the wisdom of God, Jesus taught the people about what they had forgotten. He taught by example and in real time, by demonstrating love, compassion, tolerance, and acceptance of all people. He did, after all, walk among the rich and the poor – with equal footing no less.

He did not care about your standing in the community; Jesus cared about your standing with God. Jesus connected all of us to the source of every living thing. He did it by being an action-taker, a preacher, and through the words that He spoke. His words were given as lessons for each of us to learn from, the parables spoken in a way to leave a lasting impression.

I have been guided to understand that the teachings of Jesus were given to us in parables for a reason. I believe that it was done as a way to make us dig deep and think for ourselves. This is where we can each apply the lessons given by Jesus to our own lives, and where we see fit. You see, His words resonate differently for each of us because we are all in a different state of awareness.

That is what made Jesus a teacher among teachers. He spoke the words, and we learned through our own understanding of what those words meant to us.

So, when you go about your day, and you reflect upon your life today, know that your connection to God is established through your own heart.

We were given a master teacher, his name is Jesus, and His love does not discriminate. It is a love that encompasses all of mankind. If we could each get back to the truth of His birth, we could then understand the destination of His influence...

Inspired writing, July 15, 2014

Author's Reflections

My only reflections are these...

Where in your own life has Jesus made His presence known? Write your thoughts down and within your journal if you have one. This is where you can reflect on His influence.

THE GARDEN OF GETHSEMANE

"Spiritual practices are important for every soul as they forge and reinforce the connection home to source.

Your practices can come in many forms, but they will all lead you to a form of prayer. Know that it is through your prayers where you can all speak with God.

Remember this Dear Ones, if your desire to commune is a solitary one, or that of fellowship, just know that each spiritual practice achieves the same purpose."

I love this message because it simply states that all roads lead to Rome, or in this case, home. It does not matter how you choose to worship, because the link created goes straight to source.

Jesus sat within the Garden of Gethsemane where He taught His disciples how to pray and meditate. It was through meditation that He taught them the way to connect directly with God, just as He did. It was in this garden where Jesus prayed the evening before His Crucifixion. His only desire was to be one with the Father.

In closing, it doesn't matter if you choose to walk in nature, meditate or sit in a church – each is a guidepost that will lead you to your own inner peace. This is where your prayers are heard, happiness is achieved, and prayers are answered in one way or another.

Channeled and Inspired Writing, August 14, 2014

Author's Reflections

Most people have a spiritual avenue that they have chosen to travel. It is through those travels that they tap into the divine part of self.

For those of you looking to deepen your connection with God, the greatest path is through meditation. Jesus was the teacher of this modality for His disciples. Meditation is how He taught them to practice mindfulness and guided them to where they could go to clearly hear the voice of God.

This is where you too can tap into the resources that have always been available to you. Practice makes perfect, so if you are new to meditation be patient with yourselves.

For the novice, there are plenty of wonderful, guided meditations to follow and learn from. Just do your research and see which spiritual teacher you are drawn to. This is where you can investigate their methods of meditation and where you will find a resonance with one of them, I am sure of this.

To be spiritual is one thing, to be an active participant is another. As you find a resonance with your daily ritual you will most likely be drawn to creating your own sacred space in which to worship.

JESUS THE TEACHER

Jesus was and is an example for all to follow, as His teachings transcend all religions and cultures, and where they speak to the heart of man and not at him. Jesus is the living example of love and forgiveness personified. During His life, He was pure of heart, detached from the physical trappings of the human condition, and taught us from a place of understanding.

The teachings of Jesus continue to touch our lives daily as He becomes an example of God's love for us. This is why we feel so deeply when we love or even when we are hurting. It is because Jesus became the living example of God's love, and it must never be forgotten.

Next time you are quick to anger and hold onto grudges, ask yourself why. Next time you cast aspersions and judgement upon your fellow man, know that he is doing the best that he can. Know that he can only put forth into this world what he has been taught from those who came before him.

Next time you decide to withhold your love from another, know that you are withholding love from yourself as well.

"Be the example for others to follow, for as you give and you do so freely, know that it will be returned back to you one-hundred-fold.

Take a moment and give reverence to those you admire like Jesus, Buddha, Loa Tzu. Learn from the teachings of the masters, and as you do, apply their teachings to your own lives daily.

*When you can do this, it is then that you yourself
become a beacon of light for others to follow."*

Channeled and Inspired Writing, September 3, 2014

Author's Reflections

Each of you reading these words are teachers of your own life's experiences. They are the platform from which you can literally change another person's life. It is after all what you teach that matters most, as lessons of the heart are most often the ones that are deeply felt.

Take a moment to recall when you once stood before someone who was able to guide you from a place of experience. Look to this experience and see where you may have shared it with another person.

See the ripple effect it has created from a single pebble tossed into the pond. It is from this perspective, that you can fully understand the message written above and become a teacher of this wisdom.

DEAR GOD

"Dear God, return me to my center, to the core of my own voice of reason, the voice of my own understanding. Do this, so that I may hear Your divine guidance as I travel the path of light that is laid before my own two feet.

When I find myself within fear's grip because my way is not like any others, remind me that it is not supposed to be. Do this so that I may find the courage to allow my own uniqueness to carry me forth.

Dear God, fill my heart with Your pure light and love, so that when I stand upon holy ground I can understand my own place within this physical world, my own place within this spiritual journey. Do this so that I never doubt the validity of such things as Your grace bathes me in its light."

This is a beautiful prayer, and it is a reminder of how to navigate your way within a world of many. These words of beauty and truth empower each of us to stand within our own power, strong and steady, and within our own light. This is where we allow the divine hand of God's will to work through us, as we navigate this human life.

These words become the reminder that, yes, the foundations have been poured. This becomes the platform from which we stand and apply the teachings that we take on as our own truth. This is where we must recognize that these lessons are only an aspect of who we truly are. It is when we allow ourselves to think outside of the box, that we will begin to see our own place within all things.

Today is the day to acknowledge that your place within this world is realized when you understand that you each shine in your own unique way.

Channeled and Inspired Writing, September 30, 2014

Author's Reflections

Individuality is what comes to mind here, and it is when we stretch our wings outwards that we can begin to soar. The only way to do so is to not be frightened of leaving the nest and flying solo. When you are brave enough to fly, your purpose is ignited and where you take flight.

FORGIVENESS

"Thank those who have wounded you and use the scars
as a reminder of the gift, for without your own
suffering, you could never know your own joy.

Heal the wound and you heal the heart, for one cannot
happen without the other. When you are hurting, I am
hurting too, for I clearly see the suffering of your soul.

I give to you a brand-new sunrise every day as an
offering of my eternal love for you.

Use it to warm your body, nourish your soul, and find
refuge in its light, for in the reflection of the sun lies
your own salvation."

Forgiveness is the message delivered by the Master known as Jesus, and in this parable, He speaks of the forgiveness that He so beautifully displayed while He walked among us in the flesh and blood.

Jesus was the teacher of many different things, yet His ability to forgive, even the darkest of betrayals, is an example for all of us to follow.

Take a moment and join me in forgiving those who have hurt us, and as we do, we release the anger, judgement, and grudges towards them. These negative emotions being carried within our own hearts serve no one. They only become the things that have weighed us down.

In Jesus's name we pray, Amen.

By releasing this energy, you will gain a sense of freedom as you allow love to move in.

"Release and let it go, for this is what will serve the greatest good, and the highest joy of your own soul's light. Take this opportunity, to experience the freedom that forgiveness provides to you."

Channeled from Jesus, October 11, 2014

Author's Reflections

Oh, those tricky relationships that keep us locked in a state of despair. "He or she owes me an apology and I will never forget!"

How many of you have found yourselves saying those painful words? This state of perpetual anger can keep us trapped for an eternity.

Here is what we can do to let it go and move on.

Try to find forgiveness for them. Learn that letting it go benefits you most. Wishing them well and wishing them away helps to break the ties that bind you. Take a moment and reflect on this before you move on. Who might you need to forgive, or better yet, who do you need forgiveness from?

Anger is a double-edged sword, and as they say it takes two to tango. So instead of having to dance to the same old song, free yourself as you find forgiveness in the situation. If you can do this for yourself, you can then be totally free to live a life without regrets.

Look to Jesus for inspiration, as He was the example of how to forgive. Even in His last breath, He forgave those who crucified him.

THE ROSARY

O ur Lady of Grace asks each of you to pray the Rosary as a novena for the suffering of our world.

"As you pray the Rosary, its power sends prayers to those who are in need, and have been affected by disease, poverty, and separation from Source.

Be not fearful and know that God hears all prayers, for He has not forgotten you, it is just that some have forgotten Him.

The power of prayer is a magnificent thing, and while you pray the Rosary, know that it will take you into a deep state of meditation.

Your prayer becomes the guidepost, at the crossroads, between faith and doubt.

It is your choice in which way to travel, as one way is illuminated in light, the other in darkness.

Say your prayers today, for there are many souls who can benefit from your selflessness."

Channeled from the Blessed Mother, October 17, 2014

Autor's Reflection

It was 1991, and a man named Joe R. was holding prayer vigils in an Illinois cemetery called Queen of Heaven. I was privileged to attend some of these vigils, where we would pray the Rosary. As we all gathered together, he would communicate with the Holy Mother. I can tell you this: when he was in communion with Her, the air temperature would be warm and still, even on the coldest winter's day.

I have had three visitations from the Blessed Mother, and the one I am about to share happened after I received a phone call from my sister. Joe, she said, had asked that we pray for those in purgatory because the Blessed Mother requested us to do so. I asked her, "What is purgatory?" and she told me it is a place where souls get stuck. "That is impossible," I replied, but my need to know more got the best of me. She told me that after some people die, they need prayers to get them out of purgatory. I asked what else the Blessed Mother had told Joe, and she said nothing — we just needed to pray.

I began praying to Our Lady as soon as we hung up the phone. I asked to know more about purgatory; I also did as my sister requested and prayed that all souls in purgatory be lifted into heaven.

It was a few weeks later when Our Lady of Grace appeared to me in my dream state. In the dream I was in a gymnasium, and she appeared near the back entrance. She was dressed in blue and white, and a soft glow surrounded her. As she stood looking at me, I noticed she had something in her hand. She told me she was going to show me heaven, purgatory, and hell. She then stretched out her hand towards me, in it was an olive branch. She asked me to take hold of the branch and she would show me the way.

Just like Ebenezer Scrooge in A Christmas Carol, *I was taken to three dimensions. In each I was shown God's Grace and Mercy. I was not frightened, even as we traveled at the speed of light. Next is the account of what I was shown.*

Heaven is where all souls go; it is filled with love and with much light. She showed me that there is not one soul that is turned away. She assured me that it does not take any special favor to go to heaven, because in God's eyes all souls are created equal.

Purgatory is a place where souls who are in need of healing go. They enter purgatory through The Gates of Heaven and are taken to rooms filled with different colored lights for healing. This is where we are asked to pray for those souls who have no one else to pray for them. It is not a punishment like we are taught by the church, but a place where souls in need are lifted up by God's Grace.

Hell, as she showed me, resides within the minds of all people. It is a place created by the human being while living in the flesh, which is where all true suffering occurs. She showed me that the fire and brimstone is just an illusion created by those whose choices are marred by self-destruction.

Praying the Rosary was taught to me by my mother. I respect it because I see the power in the prayer requests being made by the petitioner. Our Lady asks us to pray the Rosary as a way to lift those up who are suffering and in need. It is a way to pray on a universal level for all souls, in this world, or the next.

If praying the Rosary is not your thing, you can use mala beads. It is just another way to spend a longer time in prayer, with the beads serving as the roadmap towards the same destination.

OUR LADY OF GRACE...

O ur Lady of Grace asks us to take refuge in the arms of Christ today.

"As you take refuge today, paint your doorways and those of your families with the symbolic Blood of Christ, so that scourge and plague may pass you by.

For those who believe in Him also believe in God the Father, maker of Heaven and Earth, for all things given can also be taken away.

You must pray for the suffering of many, and when asking to be healed, know that the heart must be healed first. This is the order in which to heal the body, for it is through your heart that you receive His grace.

Today is a reminder, to find strength in that which you cannot see, and know that it is your faith that will return you home.

The pathway for the faithful is through the Body of Christ, as He becomes the resurrection and the promise of everlasting life.

Say a prayer for all of the people of this world today, and as you pray for them, know that you pray for yourselves too."

Channeled from The Blessed Mother Mary,
October 24, 2014

Author's Reflections

As I reflect here, I am also drawn to the words "…for all things given can also be taken away." My interpretation of these words is this: It seems that some people have turned away from God and during this time we have seen much strife across the globe.

America, for instance, is being burned from within her borders. We have the powerful fanning the flames in an attempt to manipulate the masses so that they can maintain control over them. In essence, they have chosen to be like the Pharaoh who used the people's own fear against them.

It brings me back to the days of Moses and when the Pharaoh cursed all of the first-born male children to be killed. A plague came across the land and the people screamed in horror. Moses told Joshua to paint the doorways with lamb's blood. It was those doorways, painted with the symbolic Blood of Christ, that were passed over by death. It was faith that had delivered these people through the night and proved to the Pharaoh the power of God's will be done. In the end, the Pharaoh, in word and in deed, had cursed his own house, where his son died.

The more we pull away from our creator, the greater the strife created. It has happened because we have forgotten the sacrifice Jesus made for us.

I would say, put your own hateful feelings towards others, even those who have delivered us into bondage aside. Pray that their hearts be opened to receive God's Grace and Mercy. This is where we begin to heal all hearts on a mass level, including our own.

When we cloak ourselves in this energy, we symbolically paint our doorways with the Blood of Christ. This is where we find solace in our faith and allow our faith to lead the way.

Heeding this prayer will lead you towards self-healing and reminds you that all things are possible through Christ.

PRAYER

"As you take a moment to pray and you thank God for your many blessings, I ask that you pray for all of the souls who inhabit the earth. Pray that there may be peace and harmony among all nations and all people.

Please include in your prayers a blessing for your sweet Mother Earth as well, for as she gives to you, you must also give back to her.

I want you to remember that when you pray for another, you not only elevate your own vibration, but you also elevate the vibration of the souls that you include within your prayer of good intentions."

I had a beautiful aunt; her name was Dorothy. She was very devoted to the power of prayer. Her faith in God and her religion was the rock that we all leaned upon when in need of an extra blessing. It was her faith and belief in God's Grace that I believe drew extra favor from God when she prayed. Why? Because her faith never wavered.

My Aunt Dorothy had a list of people written within the pages of her bible, and each day she would pray for those souls. The rosary that I have was made from the flowers that were placed upon her casket as we wished her safe travels back home.

So, in honor of her devotion to God, I honor her in this book. She touched not only my life, but the lives of everyone who were lucky enough to have known her.

"It is most import to never forget to include yourself in your prayers, as this is where God can intervene with a Grace in your favor."

Channeled and Inspired Writing, November 2, 2014

Author's Reflections

How you pray does not matter — why? Because it is your intent behind your prayers that has the ability to change all things.

THE GOLDEN LIGHT
OF THE CHRIST CONSCIOUSNESS

The Golden Light of the Christ Consciousness was shown to me by a beautiful girl in spirit in February 1993 while I vacationed in Mexico with family and friends.

Around four a.m. I was awoken from my slumber by a strange feeling. There was an energy that had filled the room with the vibration of sound. I opened my eyes and gazed around the room, now illumi-nated in a golden light.

I could see all things with clarity, including the two beds in the room and the people who were asleep within them. Suddenly, my eyes were drawn to the steps on the platform near the end of both beds. There was a young girl standing there, gazing at me from the top of the landing. As she stood there, I could see her clearly but felt unafraid.

She had two ponytails that hung just past her chin, her bangs cut short, just above her doe-like eyes. She wore a flowered skirt with suspenders over her shoulders, and a short-sleeved white shirt tucked into the skirt. She had on black patent leather shoes, with white socks folded over at the top, in her arms she was clutching a ragdoll.

As our eyes locked, she proceeded to walk down the steps, making her way to my side of my bed. She stood there, glowing, and smiling softly at me. There were no words spoken between us, only Universal Wisdom which was passed from her and onto me. It seemed as if time stood still.

As I reached out to touch her, she vanished, taking the golden hue along with her, but leaving the memory of her visit for me to carry forward always. This young girl who materialized before my conscious eyes is a gift that I will cherish for life.

The gift from this visitation is the vibration of the Golden Light. It is an energy that I use when calling upon Spirit to work with and through me. It is also the energy that I use to teach from.

It has a different vibration than just white light. The Golden Light is the color, or aura if you will, that you will see surrounding Christ and other Ascended Masters and Teachers. Its vibration carries its own intelligence as it lifts your spirit to ascend a bit higher.

If you allow yourself, you too can experience this Golden Light. Just for a moment, close your eyes and surrender to the possibility.

Close your eyes and breathe. See yourself being bathed in a beautiful golden light. Its energy is warm and loving; it feels like liquid silk upon your skin. Continue to breathe, drawing the light in and through you so that it touches every fiber and cell within your being. This light is that of the Christ Consciousness. Now, just sit for a moment longer and within its power. This is where you become acquainted with the Light of Christ and where you begin to see yourself transformed.

I encourage each of you to call upon the Golden Light when doing your spiritual work, and like a waterfall it will cascade down and upon you as it lifts you up to new heights.

Inspired Writing, November 18, 2014

Author's Reflections

This is an opportunity to just sit and breathe. This is when you can tap into The Christ Consciousness and expand your horizons so to speak. The Golden Light, in my opinion, is connected to the evolution of the soul. And isn't that what we all strive for? To evolve and move closer to the Oneness?

Take a moment before you move on, to play with the energy of transformation and allow yourselves to awaken just a bit more. It is through your own awakening that your purpose has the opportunity to make its presence known.

THE MIRACLE OF CHRIST

"Jesus was conceived through the Holy Ghost, born of the Virgin Mary to share with each of you God's Grace. He was a Master Teacher, Healer, Prophet, an example of Pure Love and more. His teachings are echoed throughout all religions, races, and nations as His love for each of you is limitless.

Jesus, through His own earthly lifetime, walked among all people from rich to poor, beggar to thief. Sharing with all of mankind His ability to see beyond the human experience and expose the beauty in each soul that He encountered.

It was through Him that God's Love for you was given a platform to shine from.

Pray for peace, and for God's grace to shine upon all people, all nations, so that we may heal the hearts of those who are hurting along with yourselves.

This is the way to bring to each of you, a greater understanding of God's love for you."

Channeled from my Council, November 30, 2014

Author's Reflections

Jesus and His ministry, His words, and His wisdom are just as meaningful today as they were when He walked among us. This channeled message is a testament to who He was.

He gave us a roadmap to follow in scripture and beyond. It is up to each of us to decide how we follow that roadmap.

Just for a moment, stop and think about your lifetime. Reflect on where Jesus has left the biggest impression within your own life. This way you can see how that single impression becomes multifaceted. Just like a diamond has many faucets of light, see just where the light is shining the brightest. This way you can see the depth of the diamond and where you still have other avenues to grow in Him.

THE TEACHERS OF OUR LIFETIME

"Teachers, teach me so that I may learn and grow, but let me not lean upon you as a crutch as I know that this will only cripple me.

Teachers, bless me with a solid foundation to build upon, so that when I need to learn from another what you cannot give to me now, I will have the platform to build upon.

Teachers, share with me your wisdom so that it then becomes my wisdom too. Yet help me to understand that you are only a part of my growth, as the rest is up to me.

Teachers, teach me so that I may grow from the seeds of your knowledge which are planted within the garden of my own life."

We will all have many teachers throughout our lifetime; some living, and some we have only read about in books like Jesus and Buddha. We will each take what we have need of and leave what does not resonate behind.

Each of you will, just as I have done, seek out that which you are in need of. This is where you will realize that the teachers you are seeking can be found. Through discernment, you may also realize that you only need a little from one teacher and a bounty from another. Why? Because one becomes the cornerstone of your beliefs and the others become the steppingstones on which to briefly walk.

Jesus, in my opinion, is the example of this cornerstone where all people can learn and grow from.

On this journey of learning each of you will find your core teacher, and it is from this core that your foundation is formed. This is an important part of your growth and where a solid structure of principle and ethics becomes the platform for you to build upon.

"Each child must be given order and discipline to learn from, yet it must be built upon a foundation of love. For if it is not built upon love, then that foundation will only crumble beneath their feet.

This is the core of your teaching and the standard that each of you should adhere to. Learn all that you can from each teacher that you are fortunate enough to sit with, as they will help to awaken the sleeping part of your own soul's light."

This channeled wisdom from Spirit applies to our lives, from birth to adulthood. Apply them as you see fit, and you will see your own place as the teacher of this wisdom.

Channeled and Inspired Writing, December 1, 2014

Author's Reflections

We have many teachers who will grace our path, from our parents to our schoolteachers; from our religious leaders to our spiritual gurus; from our bosses to our peers; and from our brothers to our sisters.

They come to teach us what we are hungry for. It is from their own table that they will share that bounty with you. It is from that bounty where you are fed.

Take a moment to reflect on the teachers of your own lifetime. See how, where, and when they shaped your human existence. See the good, the bad, and the indifferent in each of them.

Even when the teacher falls short, they do so as a way for you to learn. This is where discernment comes into play. It is up to you to know when to take what you have need of and move on.

The same rules apply when a teacher has lifted you up. No one teacher is the be-all and end-all for any student. But when you find that one who has taught you how to fly, it is up to you to fly. This is when you thank the teacher for giving you wings, and where you give them the freedom to lift up another.

HEAVEN

What happens to our soul when we cross over and enter the gates of heaven? Heaven is just another name for the Spirit World, and we will all transition there eventually. Rest assured that when your soul walks through the pearly gates you will be greeted by many. There will be some there who you will know by name and some whose soul energy you will recognize from other lifetimes; this is called your soul group. Along with the familiar faces and energies of your soul group, your angels, guides, and teachers are also waiting there to assist you in your transition.

As you enter the spirit realm, you are instantly prepared for your life's review. This is a graduation of sorts, and when you get to see and feel every aspect of the life you just left. It is a tool for your soul to learn from and as a way to show you where you excelled in life and where you may have fallen short. Your soul's journey has been recorded and is now added to your book of life called the Akashic Records. This becomes a reference point for your soul to access at any time. Its wisdom becomes a part of your soul's blueprint for an eternity, where each lifetime can be reviewed for purposes of growth.

When you have completed your life review, and have seen your own soul's growth, you will be taken into a "Hall of Souls" by your guide. This is where you will sit with others who vibrate at the same level as you do. It is in this room that your soul will spend some time for healing purposes. This is done as a way to help your soul assimilate to the frequency of a new dimension and release your ties to the earth plane. When you look around this room you will notice that there is a common theme, a core color. This is the vibration of the souls within this room and where you will vibrate together in a sea of light and love.

When your soul is ready to move on, your guide will take you to the level that matches your soul's vibration. This is where you move into your next stage of learning, as you seek that oneness with God. This is an extremely exciting time for your soul. It is where you climb a ladder, though you can only climb as high as your soul has evolved. Once you step off the ladder you will enter a room – a floor. This is where your new stage of learning begins.

This is what Jesus referred to when he said:

"My Father's house has many rooms and I am going to prepare a place for you to stay."

This place is the next stop along the way. This is where your soul gets the opportunity to continue to learn and to grow, so that you can climb to the next rung on the ladder.

So, as you can see, the soul is eternal and never dies. It just moves on from one dimension and into the next, always preparing itself for its next sojourn. Each of us are in a constant state of evolution and indeed our soul yearns for that expansion. Your life now is only one stop of many along the way. It is important to remember that your soul has a purpose, a destiny, and a life to live. It has lessons to learn and an abundance of love to give, yet it can only be achieved when we shatter the illusions of the human condition.

Inspired Writing, February 2, 2015

Author's Reflections

This is a great time for you to reflect on what has already been written and see where the truth of Heaven resonates with you.

LEARNING HOW TO BEND

"Strong yet weak, level yet unbalanced at times. This is where you each will have found your footing within this world of many.

Your soul has ventured out and traveled many roads, weathered many storms, and it has delivered you to this very moment in time.

You each have the strength of a thousand men, yet you remain soft and supple, as the feminine brings balance to the masculine.

You have learned to bend and sway, like the branches of a tree, for your ability to bend keeps you from breaking.

As you emerge from the darkness of the cave, know that the storm has passed, the skies have cleared, and a new day is upon you.

Know this Dear Child, that your will is your strength, and it is through your will that you have been delivered to another day."

Channeled and Inspired Writing, February 26, 2015

Author's Reflections

When you are feeling lost, overwhelmed, and you just want to give up, where do you turn? As I recall, Jesus turned to God.

This is a great time to sit with this question and allow yourselves to see what tools you have used that have delivered you to a new day.

Where in life did you feel like you were going to break?

How did you learn to bend during that time?

How did you pick yourselves back up and dust yourselves off?

Sit with your journal if you have one and write your thoughts within it. When you review it later, you just may be surprised what has appeared on the paper.

THE WEARY TRAVELER

"Say a prayer for the weary traveler; send them energy to use as they choose, and judge not their journey. Until you can walk a mile within their shoes, you will never understand what has delivered them to walk within the shadows of this lifetime.

Remember that it only takes a single act of kindness towards another to shed a little sunshine upon what they may see as a dreary day. Remember to be grateful for what you do have, for it is through your gratitude that your blessings will multiply."

T his message speaks to the heart of our own personal struggles in life, and it is through our struggles that we learn to grow. For some, life is not always an easy road to travel. But if they can see past that which consumes them, faith and hope are there to guide them through.

Channeled and Inspired Writing, March 13, 2015

Author's Reflections

We live in a world filled with addictions, poverty, homelessness, hunger, and so many other struggles. It is from this perspective that I can see how a person could become weary, as they see no light at the end of the tunnel. It is also from their own standing in the community that judgement is passed on them, without knowing the backstory that has delivered them to one of these doorways.

How do we help those who we see as suffering or less fortunate?

This brings my thoughts to paying it forward. When we pay it forward through an act of kindness, the weary traveler is the one who benefits most from our kind gestures.

How do we help?

We help through understanding and having compassion for those who stand in the shadows and are seeking a way out. We help by doing in some form or fashion, even if it is just a prayer said in their favor.

How you pay it forward is not important here. It is from the action of doing where grace is given to all.

MARY MAGDALENE
ON THE ASCENDED MASTER

Jesus was known as a prophet as well as the Son of God. He is also recognized as an Ascended Master, whose teachings live on through the hearts of mankind. You see, Jesus touched the hearts of those who He spoke to, and He is recognized throughout the scriptures as the Lamb of God, who takes away the sins of this world. Jesus not only stands beside you, His words, His messages, burn within the hearts of all people. He helped to transform them as He elevated them through love.

"Humble is He and so should you be.

As the masses gathered from near and far to hear Him speak, it was His message which touched the hearts of many.

Jesus was a man of men, who embrace all of humanity. For all He wanted for them was to hear the Word of God, so that it would be realized within them.

His words are to be burned within your own hearts, and as you give from your heart, it is then extended through your hands, as this was a part of His teaching.

Come not from a place of ego; you must always give from a place of humility, for this is where the ego is tamed."

Channeled from Mary Magdalene, March 26, 2015

Author's Reflections

Jesus taught us humility and it is one of the greatest gifts that we can give to ourselves.

When we are humble, we in a sense push the ego aside. This is the point at which our judgments of people and situations cease to exist. This is where we do not posture for position. This is where we see each person, place, and even each thing as neutral. This is how we create a place of equality for all who gather within our proximity.

Some may tell you that being humble is for the weak. I will tell you it takes a person of great strength to not make others feel weak within their presence. This is called elevation through love.

LET YOUR LIGHT SHINE

"If Jesus walked in the shadows, we would never have seen or known His light.

The same goes for you, as you are asked to not stand beneath the shadows of another. Your own light was never meant to be dimmed; it was always meant to shine.

Jesus stood firmly in the face of adversity, where He continued to show us the way.

It was His words which became the roadmap for all people to follow and where His heart was on display.

This was the place within Him and where He allowed love to lead the way.

The same goes for you, and as you speak your truth let it flow always from a loving heart, for vengeance has no place here."

Channeled from the Council of Nine, April 10, 2015

Author's Reflections

An eye for an eye does not apply here, as the way is created through strength in character. Jesus showed us how to be good stewards of our lives. He left a roadmap to follow, yet He also allowed the opportunity for it to be realized within you.

This is a great time to reflect on these words and to look upon your own stewardship in this ever-changing world. Love is the key here.

THE SPOKEN WORD

"Be mindful that each word that you speak, each task that you undertake, must always be done from a place of love. For those who do not yet know love's influence will continue to be thirsty."

Channeled from Jesus, May 26, 2015

Author's Reflections

As you can see, the teachings of Jesus are deep and strong. I view Him as an Ascended Master Teacher, sent forth to feed the masses. If you read between the lines of His parables, you will understand this truth for yourselves.

GOD AND THE UNIVERSE

Who is God and what is the Universe? They are two sides of the same energy, yet they are distinct from one another. God is masculine and the Universe is feminine; I refer to the Universe as the Universal Mother, for all creation contains the duality of one energy.

Let's start with God first. It is, after all, the Divine Hand of God that supports, nurtures, and loves all things that are created within the mighty Universe. Without God our Universe would be void of this love. He sent Jesus to be the messenger of His love, so that we could feel His grace within our daily lives. In essence, God sent Jesus to the living world so we could connect the dots and find our way home. It is through the power of creation within the Universal Mother that this was made possible.

God is the Love that sustains all things, and it is within this loving vibration that we were created. We become the example of God's love when we extend our hands outward. This is where we touch the world and all things in it. The secret is that the power lies within the intent of those outstretched arms of yours. If you pay attention, this is where you will see that God is very real. He is intertwined within each of you and can be felt on a deeper level when you do things from the heart center.

"God is not, nor has He ever been separate from you. God is and always has been a part of you."

The gift that God has given to each of us here is free will. This free will governs our thinking minds and belief systems. It is through the gift of free will that we are allowed to take action. This is where the intent behind our actions flow from. When we do take action, we utilize the power of creation within the dynamics of the Universal Mother.

> *"You see, it matters not what you think nor believe because God's love will never leave you, even in your darkest times."*

I see the Universe as a vast expansion of energy where all things are created, and we have many playgrounds that we will visit within Her world. You see, God gave to us the Universal Mother, where all things are capable of being manifested – good, bad, or indifferent. It was within the energy of our Universal Mother where we were created by God's love for us. The beauty here is, He allows us to explore this part of our consciousness, free of charge. God gave to us the Universe as a tool to navigate our world, and it is through the power of the Universe that we use our beliefs, thoughts, feelings, and emotions to manifest all things tangible.

> *"Whatever it is that you desire is yours, as God gives freely to you, yet it is through the power of your own actions that will create your current reality, with the help of the Universe of course."*

The beauty of free will is that we get as many chances as we need to get it right. This is where we are guided by God, the Father, who gives us the opportunity to create within the playground of the Universal Mother. In my eyes, our free will is considered a grace, and it is through this grace that we are granted freedom of choice. God's love for us allows us the freedom to use this Universe as we see fit. This is what you would call living a human life, sustained by God's love.

"God will never close the door on you. His forgiveness and love for you allows you freedom of choice, as your soul evolves and grows within the loving arms of the Universal Mother.

Take what you have need of and leave the rest behind, for the Universe is vast, and she gives to you daily opportunities to grow within her. Yet it is your loving God that gives you the strength to move forward in your journey home."

Channeled and Inspired Writing, June 25, 2015

Author's Reflection

I would like to break it down like this. The Universal Mother is the egg, and we fertilize this egg when we desire to create. You see, God gave us fertile ground in which to grow new things. Yet it is up to each of us to sow the seeds, or in this case fertilize the egg, so that new life can be birthed within the Universal Mother's arms.

We, through the aspect of God's divine hand, become the masculine, and when we join forces with the feminine, (i.e., Universal Mother) creation happens. God allows us a playground to dabble within, and like all relationships we leave a tangible expression of our creations within it.

CHOICE IS A GIFT

Choice is a gift that each of us are privileged to use, and it is through our own free will that we have the opportunity to experience choice in all aspects of our lives.

You see, there is no rulebook that holds all the available choices we can pick from; rather, it is our own moral compass that will lead us down the pathway of right or wrong. It is through trial and error that we create our own guidelines to live by. This is where we must each be mindful of our own thoughts, deeds, and actions towards another as we live freely by our own choices made.

"Judge not another for the choices that they make, as it is not your place to govern another's life."

Each of us must find a way to accept others as they are, for it is through your acceptance that they can peacefully navigate their own way, while you give yourself the opportunity to do the same. This is what Jesus did; He spoke to the hearts of those who followed Him, then allowed the people to choose for themselves.

You see, we are all created by one common thread, and that thread is made of pure love. As we are raised, we have each been given a standard to live by which becomes a part of our belief system. This is the place from which we make our choices. As we move through time, it becomes a roadmap to reflect upon.

As I reflect here, the words of Jesus stand out, "Judge not another lest ye be judged." Other popular catchphrases, such as "Make love, not war" that were said in the 1960s, seems to be a spin on those same words.

These words spoken by Jesus are more than just words; they are simple yet powerful principles for us to live by. We have no right to judge or even tell another how to live their lives. Why? Because it is not for us to dictate their path through the choices that we desire them to make. We must remain mindful that it is up to them to find their own way in which to navigate this world.

I will leave you with these words from my Council:

"Live a peaceful life always as love becomes the guidepost, the lamplight, upon your own path in life. This is where you will each be blessed beyond measure."

Channeled and Inspired Writing, June 27, 2015

Author's Reflections

Choices, there are so many to make. That is the beauty about being a human in a tangible world. We get so many things to choose from.

There are some choices that we like, and some we wish we would have never made. The question is, are all choices created equal? I would say they sure are, because those choices are what have molded you into who you are today.

Is there still something to learn about yourselves from the choices that you have made? Again, I would say yes! But in order to see them, you first must be willing to look.

Take a moment to go down memory lane and see which choices have made the greatest impact upon your life today. Good, bad, or indifferent – all of your choices matter. As you can see, you have three options to play with here. This is a great time to be completely honest with yourself. It gives you an opportunity to bring those memories to the surface and allow each of them to teach you from a place in your past.

This is a good time to get out that journal and do a little soul-searching.

A MOMENT OF REFLECTION...

I was fortunate enough to take a class taught by a famous medium from New York. On this day he spoke so beautifully about The Christ and His teachings that I felt as if he were revealing common ground, a place of communion that we both understood on a soul level.

He also spoke of Buddha and referenced his Zen Master through-out his morning lecture. He was giving us all a pathway towards enlightenment while acknowledging our freedom to choose it, only if we desired to do so. Throughout his lecture I had been listening in fascination; then, suddenly I sat up in my chair, my ears opened wide. This was the moment I gained an understanding of who he truly was. The foundation of his teaching revealed, the structure which had been built beneath his own two feet, the platform on which he now stood.

There were many things that this famous medium spoke of as he channeled the information. He allowed the words of wisdom to flow freely from him as they saturated the room and the hearts of all who were present.

One thing in particular really struck a chord with me. It was a quote from his Zen Master.

"You have to be Fierce as you walk your own path."

I understood this as a knowingness within me, *"that you have to own it, and there is "No" in between, for this is the path to awaken that which sleeps within you."* The words that were spoken filled my own heart in such a way that I understood them to mean; *"fear has no place here."*

Jesus spoke often to the crowds during his life, and He asked them to *"Fear Not."* He also asked them to have faith and reminded them that *"I Am with you."*

As I continued to reflect, I understood that those who get wrapped up in the emotional state of being, keep their own awakening from occurring. They continue to walk in fear's shadow, for they have not yet allowed trust to lead the way. You see, it takes great courage, trust, and an internal leap of blind faith to walk the path of your own soul's light. This is where you lay bare your soul for all the world to see. Once you understand your own place within the walk, fear can no longer lead the way, as it is through your own fierceness that God's Will be done.

So, for today as I share my own fierceness with each of you, I do so as a way to inspire you to step from the shadows just as the Christ did, and allow your own truth to be revealed.

Inspired Writing, October 4, 2015

Author's Reflections

How is God's Will done through you?

Where have you stood in the face of adversity like Jesus had done and allowed your own truth to be seen and heard?

What time in your own lives has your fierceness made an appearance and how were you empowered by it?

If none of these things have occurred due to fear's influence, then this would be a great time to face those fears.

What are you fearful of?

Reflect on these questions and learn something awesome about yourself. Acknowledge the fierceness in you, or the lack thereof, to see where your potential resides.

Get those journals out and begin writing!

INNER PEACE

As I sat again in the classroom of this famous medium from New York, he posed the following to the group:

Question of The Christ

"If you do not seek peace, then what is it that you are seeking"?

I would like to give you my interpretations of the answer to this question; it comes from a perspective of my own understanding as I navigate my internal truth. I also encourage you to do the same.

Too many people seek outside of themselves for happiness, joy, love and even wealth. They have not yet understood that what they are seeking is right inside them, and always has been. When people begin posturing for position, they lose sight of that inner peace and begin to run on the hamster wheel of life.

When a person chooses to hold onto anger over joy, sadness over happiness, or hate over love, inner peace eludes them. When they are willing to do anything to be at the top of their game, they may only feel the thorns of injustice, rather than breathing in the sweet fragrance of peace.

Ultimately, you will stay on that hamster wheel as long as you choose any road that voids your inner peace. This outward reaching by you, however, is only a part of the human experience and where you choose to continue navigating unchartered waters.

Jesus reminds us that, *"The Kingdom of God is within you."*

In the words of my Council:

"It is the cycle of doubt that keeps them from enjoying the fruits of their already earned successes."

From this point forward I encourage you to begin enjoying your life right now. This includes what you deem as your successes and where you can learn from your own shortcomings. When you can learn to be comfortable within your own skin and enjoy your own experience without compromise, you will begin to see the bigger picture. It is not about what you look like or what you have; it is about who you are in this exact moment in time, because all the rest really does not matter anyways.

Inner peace is not that difficult to find, yet it takes great effort on your part to do the work toward it. Until you find that inner peace and learn that life is not a competition with others, you will continue to seek outside of yourself. You will avoid going internal for the answers and wonder why peace has continued to elude you.

Jesus taught us how to seek, but the direction of the seeking is up to the seeker. As any good teacher will do, He will point out the way, yet it is up to the student to open the door.

So, for today, know this:

"Peace is yours today and always, yet it is up to you to access it for yourself. The path before you is a simple one that can only be realized once you have placed your own foot upon it."

Channeled and Inspired Writing, October 7, 2015

Author's Reflections

Question of The Christ:

"If you do not seek peace then what is it that you are seeking"?

Where has the cycle of doubt kept you from enjoying inner peace?

What outdated patterns of learned behavior have kept you in a holding pattern when it comes to inner peace?

If you have experienced inner peace, what has it taught you about yourself and life in general?

Take a moment to explore these questions. Write your own reflections within your journal. This is where you can see where inner peace resides for you.

AS JESUS FEEDS YOU

"There are many lights that will be fed from one table, yet what they eat from that table then becomes a part of their own truth. You see, it is by one single thread that many are fed, and those who ate from the table of the soul known as Jesus, took from His teachings and made them their own.

After each feast, the bounty was then shared, and where each soul was given a basket of their own to nourish other souls from. It was a way to feed the masses, through the wisdom gained from one supper, that was shared between them on that night.

Please know that as each soul shares with another, wisdom is gained from eating off the plate of one. It is from here that it is transformed into the words of their own soul's understanding, lessons delivered from their own unique perspective.

You see Dear Ones, as one teaches, another gains, and what they have gained is a pearl of wisdom, a pearl of truth. Once the light shines upon the truth, it can never be dimmed, as the light is designed to show each of you the way home."

The message is clear today, and it is a beautiful one at that. As I see it, we have each eaten from the table of Christ's Wisdom. As He fed the masses during His short lifetime, His words would influence the lives of many. He has touched all religions, all people with the word of God. He taught us what it means to know God's love and how to access it for ourselves. He taught us many things, but please know this:

"The Kingdom of Heaven is within you. The way to access Heaven is through love's doorway. You are never far away from God's Divine Grace. When you enter to ask God to grant you a favor, please do so from the wisdom of your own heart's doorway, as it is through the heart center where His grace is given unto you. Know that each of you will touch so many in this lifetime and what you leave with each soul will also be carried within you for an eternity." ~ Jesus

Channeled by my Council, Jesus and Inspired Writing October 24, 2015

Author's Reflections

As my father was in his final transition home, I took a moment to sit with him alone. It was a time to speak from my heart and let him know how I felt. I spoke these words to him just before he passed.

"Dad, know that you have taught all of your children how to fish and because of you none of us will ever go hungry."

My dad did not have a religious practice when we were growing up, but he was known to quote the bible often. He taught us so much about life, survival, and a solid work ethic. He gave us the tools we needed to navigate life. But it was up to each of his children to pick up those tools and to use them. We each learned in our own way how to do these things by watching him.

The same goes for knowing God. Jesus showed us the way, yet it is up to each person to access the doorway on their own.

In your own reflections, how have you accessed the Kingdom of Heaven within you, and where have you shared that doorway with others?

GOD CAN ONLY INTERCEDE
WHERE MAN WILL ALLOW

"There is so much power in prayer yet know that God cannot intercede where men will not allow.

It is the free will of those fighting that interferes with His divine hand reaching in, to change the actions of those who cannot see beyond the illusion of the cause.

You see, God gave to each of you free will to use as you choose. It is a gift afforded to each soul that is born to this world.

When people decide to lay down their own swords, it is then that peace will overcome this nation."

Channeled by the Council November 27, 2015

Author's Reflections

The time is upon us now to do just that, lay down our swords and unite.

The separation amongst all people is just astounding when you think about it.

The question is, How did we get here, and how do we move forward?

I would like you to know that there will never be a battle that serves anything other than your own ego. When unchecked, the ego can wield a mighty sword. This sword not only wounds another, but it also cuts deeply into the one who holds the hilt.

A time of reflection on the battles that we have waged will allow each of us to see the wounds that have been opened within ourselves and another.

THE PLANTED SEEDS

"There are no two souls who will communicate to the world in the same exact way. Yet it is what each person gathers along the way that becomes a part of the platform that they will find themselves working from. It is through the uniqueness of their own soul's light that makes it so.

Each person who steps into their own power has the ability to share it with the world around them. This is, after all, the sacred part of their own soul's language. Yet be mindful that not everyone you encounter will quite understand your way, and that is okay.

We know that it takes great courage and strength to stand within the light of your own soul's wisdom. It is from this platform, and in full illumination, that you can no longer hide from the world.

It will feel as if you have the strength of a thousand men supporting you, as you deny nothing and embrace everything."

The Council of Nine

I am in awe of how each soul captures, and displays, a natural, beautiful synchronicity with its own essence and wisdom.

Jesus is the perfect example of this truth. He was fully illuminated for the whole world to see as He placed His heart on display. He did this so that His disciples and the people could learn about the way.

Jesus knew that if He planted the seeds within the garden of His disciples' hearts the harvest would multiply. He shared with them in a way that they could each translate His wisdom, from their own place of understanding.

You see, your own path may not be the path that others choose to follow, yet with grace and dignity we must find a way to honor the journey of each human being who passes us by.

When Peter denied Jesus for the first of three times, just before Jesus's arrest, he did so, not because he didn't love Him. Peter denied Jesus because he did not, at that time, possess the courage to stand within the truth of his own soul's light. This is why he stood silently as he watched the man he called Rabbi, die on the cross. In the end, however, Peter found his voice and the strength to stand before all people, to speak of a truth that resonated so deeply within him.

It was in Peter's own perfect timing that this awakening had occurred, as the words of Jesus resonated within his heart. This is what gave him the strength and a platform to work from, as the foundation, through the teachings of Jesus, were laid so beautifully beneath his feet.

Jesus's words to His disciples before He was arrested were these:

"If the world hates you, keep in mind that they hated me first."

This was Jesus's way to give His disciples the strength to carry on after His death. He knew that they would be standing in the face of adversity as they carried on His ministry and preached about the man called Jesus.

"The courage to be honest with yourself and others will present itself when you allow God to hold your hand. This is where you will each stand illuminated, in the truth of your own soul's light. As you do, all the beauty that resides within you is then amplified. It takes great courage and strength to not deny who you are, and what you were born to do. As the fears within you subside, you are left only with the truth." ~ Jesus

Channeled from Jesus, My Council and Inspired Writing, January 6, 2016

Author's Reflections

In my classes I teach people about embracing their own truth. I tell them that I am just a light who helps to amplify the light within them. I help to lead them to the doorway of that light, but it is up to each person to open the door and step across the threshold for themselves.

It takes great courage to speak your own truth. Why? Because not everyone will embrace what so deeply resonates within you. Your truth becomes a seed that can be planted within the hearts of others, but it is up to each person to water that seed as they find a way to take aspects of your truth on as their own.

Just be mindful of this: as each teacher crosses your path, they will become a reflection of your own light. It is from those reflections where you can see your own place within the work at hand. It is not your job to become a carbon copy of those teachers. It is your job to take what you have learned from them and make it your own.

Who have been the most influential teachers of your own life?

How have they helped you to stand in the authenticity of this light?

These are important questions to reflect on as you validate your own growth thus far. Jesus becomes the example of this truth.

SAY A LITTLE PRAYER FOR ME

"It is not what you say nor what you do that will change anyone. For change is a natural progression of the individual person who is in need of change's influence.

Please know that it is when the person is ready to change that they will step forth to drink from change's cup, and not a moment beforehand.

No person, nor higher power, can ever infringe upon the free will of the learning soul. Yet prayer does assist and will elevate those in need of your prayers.

God does hear all prayers, and He feels your yearnings when it comes to another soul. Yet it is when the soul who is in need of your prayers becomes open to receiving them, that change can occur.

Prayers are in a sense energy, sent by one person on behalf of another. This is the simple path through which prayers are delivered and received.

Please know that your prayers do assist in the transformation of the soul in need, as they move from one state of being and into the next. It is when this transformation occurs that miracles happen, and where your prayers become answered.

This is after all, how prayer was meant to be realized by those who understand the power of prayer's impact upon your brothers and your sisters."

Channeled by the Council on March 19, 2017

Author's Reflections

Prayer is a powerful tool that can assist in the transformation of all things. It is the only thing that we can control when it comes to our desires for another. It is our way of doing something when we feel there is nothing left for us to do.

When we pray for another, we ask God to intercede on their behalf. The key here is to recognize what we are praying for. If we are praying that they change their ways, we must be mindful that change will only come when they are ready to change.

I like to pray for those I love and see struggling in this way:

Dear God, please allow the voice of _____'s own soul's wisdom to bubble to the surface so that he/she can hear clearly what will serve his/her highest good today. Wrap him/her in Your grace and lead him/her from the darkness and into the light. Help to heal the broken aspects that have led him/her down the path of his/her own suffering today.

In Jesus's name, I pray. Amen.

You can use this prayer if you would like to. Just insert their name into the prayer as you pray for them.

I would like to leave you with this, it is when you change the energy of the prayer that the prayer becomes most powerful.

THE CRUCIFIXION AND THE GRACE
OF GOD'S GLORY...

G ood Friday is the day when Christians gather and celebrate as they prepare for the Resurrection of Christ. This is what the Bible, throughout the centuries has taught us.

You see, Good Friday is the day that Jesus was scourged, beaten, and crowned with a wreath of thorns. This is when He prepared Himself for His final journey as a man of flesh and blood. This is the day when Jesus carried the cross upon His back as He was stoned by many and adored by others. His own mother Mary walked along with Him and became a witness of His sacrifice for the world.

His journey up the mount was a painful one. Jesus struggled as He felt the human body grow weaker. With each step He took He endured the sting of the whips as they flogged Him without mercy.

Jesus knew His purpose here on earth and that was to teach people the way back to God through unconditional love. With each step forward, He knew that His suffering would soon be over.

Let us not forget that Jesus was a Master Teacher, the greatest that ever walked the face of this earth. Those who understand His sacrifice for us will understand the journey of the soul's evolution.

Jesus taught us through His life's work that we are not to judge another. He set the example for us to follow as He walked among the poor and counseled the beggars. He chose to be with thieves rather than dining with sheikhs and kings, as He spoke to the hearts of the less fortunate. Jesus sat with the poor and gave of Himself freely. Through His words, he opened each person's heart to hearing the word of God.

He never turned His back on those who were suffering, and throughout His life He healed the blind, cured the sick, and raised the dead. He turned water into wine and fed the hungry with fish and bread to show God's Mercy to those who had gathered. This is where they each witnessed the miracle of God's love for them.

It was all done so that we could bear witness to God's greatness and receive the sacrifice of Jesus's life as a gift to each one of us.

Jesus taught us about faith and what it means to be faithful. Faith is the ability to believe that something is real without having to see it, as we know it to be true within our own hearts. He taught us about hope and what it means to be hopeful. He taught us about the Kingdom of Heaven and that the Kingdom resides within you.

Even as Jesus was nailed to the cross, suffering, and waiting for God to take Him home, He knew that the promise of everlasting life was to be granted to all souls. Jesus was crucified between two thieves to show the people who stood and watched that he had no power over man.

Those who crucified Him said to the people:

"If he were truly a King, he would get down off of the cross and prove his claim."

Jesus's last words before His death were *"My God, My God why have you forsaken me?"* He then drew His final breath and was released from His physical body and the suffering that He had endured as He hung upon the cross. In those moments, the skies opened up, and the earth was shaken! God's hand was shown to those who had doubted His one and only son.

Good Friday is a day to be silent and give thanks for all of your blessings as we await the celebration of his Resurrection.

Peace be with you.

Inspired Writing, March 26, 2016

Author's Reflections

Where do you find yourselves in Christ today and how does your faith sustain you?

Reflect on that and you will recognize your place in today's world.

THE POWER OF YOUR PRAYERS

Praying is such a powerful way to call upon the Heavens when we see the need for God's intervention on behalf of ourselves and others. I have seen firsthand how the power of prayer can change a life, not only for myself, but for those that I pray for as well.

Prayer was always a staple within the home that I grew up in. It taught me how to have faith in what I cannot see, and to believe that all things will be answered in some form or fashion. Prayers are said by us for a multitude of reasons, this I know. When you find yourselves praying for your family, your friends, or even yourself,

"Know that the souls of those who you pray for will always experience what they have need of."

When it comes to our prayers for others, we may at times find ourselves praying harder and harder because we want so desperately for this other person's life to be healed. But the key is this:

"The other person also has to desire the same outcome."

In the end, it is not up to us how our prayers are received. It is only when those who you are praying for become opened to your prayers that the miracles of life, and God's grace, can intercede.

"Prayer connects us to our faith; faith connects us to our God."

This is where we become immersed in the power of prayer and stand in our knowingness of what our own perception of God is. There is not one priest, guru, or spiritual teacher's perspective that governs the only ideal of who and what God is for you or for me. It is for each of us to recognize our belief in Him and to know that prayer is the gateway towards Him. It is ultimately this belief that connects us to Him and allows us to know Him in our hearts.

It is through our own ability that we recognize how God has given to each of us a way in which we choose to receive Him. It is through this avenue that we will tap into the inner knowingness of this truth for ourselves.

So, for today, know that not one prayer goes unheard or unanswered. This is where we must remember that our prayers will and do elevate the souls who are in the receipt of our offering.

Channeled and Inspired Writing, June 22, 2016

Author's Reflections

What are we praying for?

The way we pray, what we pray for, or even who we pray for are all done in the same way. We ask for the God of our understanding to intercede on our behalf. We ask for a "favor" if you will, to be granted so that we can find relief in our everyday lives.

Some of our prayers seem to be answered quickly while others seem as if they will never be answered.

Take a moment and reflect on your answered prayers. Also reflect on those prayers you are still waiting to be answered. See what or even who you have been praying for and see where the will of all comes into play.

Most often, a solitary prayer for yourselves is answered in one way or another. However, when you pray for someone else, and their will is involved, it may be stopping the flow of your good intentions. This is when you need to look at how you are praying for them.

Take yourself out of the equation and allow God's will to be done for them and their best outcome, rather than your own. This is where selflessness on your part is applied, and where you pray to elevate their own soul's voice to be heard in a way that cannot be denied by them.

In the end, it is in the way you pray that will lead you towards the good of all and not just for the good of one, yourself.

THE SEASON OF MIRACLES

Have you ever wondered why so many miracles happen around Christmastime? I believe it is because of a saturation of prayers, said by the masses on a universal level. The many prayers spoken seem to revolve around certain things which are needed, wanted, and desired. The prayers said in abundance seems to help amplify the outcomes.

"Your prayers are indeed amplified by the power of many, who are praying with the same intention, and for the same outcome as each of you are. You see Dear Ones, at this time of the year everyone's ability to manifest is amplified as they ask, believe, release, and receive."

Jesus showed us the power of this creation when He fed the masses from five loaves of bread and two fishes. Not one person went hungry on that day, as the baskets overflowed with food for all to enjoy. It all happened through the miracle of creation.

Christmas is that one time of the year when people seem to believe that they will be granted a miracle, and so the miracles seem to be granted in abundance. More people tend to manifest things through the power of creation using prayer as the vehicle. This is where the belief and magic of Santa Claus happens right before our eyes. Those tiny Christmas miracles are then wrapped in the shape of a gift and delivered on the wings of an answered prayer.

"You see Dear Ones, you each create what you desire all of the time, through your thoughts, deeds, words, and actions."

If we can learn how to harness the magic, we can then apply it to our everyday lives. This is where we would see for ourselves how those elusive Christmas miracles can be granted all year long. Due to the power of our own creation, I believe, we would then become a prosperous society.

Channeled and Inspired Writing, December 14, 2016

Author's Reflections

We have all heard the saying, "There is power in numbers." That power is real, and when we learn to harness it, we can in essence change our world for the better.

Never stop believing, never stop dreaming, and learn about the power of creation that flows from you.

I believe that it is through the Magic of Santa Claus that you can be led toward the Magic of Life.

THE GURU...OR IS HE?

I was privileged, or so I thought, to sit before a shaman from Peru and hear his words of wisdom given to a group of people on this day. I decided to share this story with you here because what I learned on this evening was a valuable lesson – definitely for me and perhaps for you as well.

As the evening began, I noticed that this man liked to be looked upon as a guru and would refer to himself as "one of the chosen few." He had handlers who would shroud him so no one else could get near when he sat before the group. This was when I recognized that he was in his ego, and though that went against my grain I kept an open mind to see what I might learn of the experience.

Throughout the evening, this man intertwined his teachings about Christ with remarks about sexual relations between a man and a woman – and in ways that were often in conflict with one another. Specifically, he implied that it was a woman's duty to satisfy a man sexually, which was off-putting to me and certainly not what I was expecting to hear from a "guru." Oddly enough, his handlers were all women.

He then spoke these words, "Deny yourself, take up your cross and follow me," which he said had been given to him by the Ascended Masters. He told us that he could not interpret what the words meant, and that no one could.

This was when I thought to myself, *"If you are to teach the world, you must have an understanding of what it is that you are trying to teach."* I then heard these words.

"Pick up pen and start writing."

I immediately began writing in my journal and was given these impressions to share. This was when my Council shared with me an interpretation of these words that the shaman said could never be interpreted by any man.

Deny Yourself

"This simply means to put your consciousness in front of your own humanness. Put the egoic mind aside and follow your own inner truth. This is where the truth is amplified within you, and where the light of God's love for all of His people resides. Let go and let God, have trust, and follow your faith."

Take up Your Cross!

"This simply means that you should speak the truth of your own soul's voice. Speak the truth of what this light is and how it came to be. Be the lightning rod that becomes the amplifier of the awakening in the hearts of others.

Be the example for others to follow, as the way is illuminated by God's Love for the Whole World."

Follow Me

"This simply means to share your own light with the world so that others will know that they too will never have to live within the shadows of darkness again. Share with them what you have come to know as the light, for it is love that keeps the home fires burning. This is where you allow yourselves the opportunity to learn and to just be."

I immediately thought to myself, is this why I was drawn to sit in this circle? Was this wisdom given to another and was the man from Peru claiming it as his own? Were the words of Christ being skewed for personal gain by him? These questions bring me to the words of Jesus that have sat with me since childhood:

"Take heed that no man deceives you. For many shall come in my name, saying, 'I am Christ'; and shall deceive many."

Remember, the teachings of Christ speak to each of us individually. On this day, I found these simple words to be immensely powerful, as they speak to the experience of each person's spiritual awakening.

True Story and Channeled from my Council, April 13, 2017

Author's Reflections

It is dangerous to look to someone as a guru. Why? Well, because you deny your own power and hand it off to someone else. Yes, people can in fact be a voice for Spirit, but even this voice can be abused through the ego of any person. This is where discernment on your part is required. It is also where you can find threads of truth. But if the energy in the form of a gut feeling makes you feel uneasy, know that it is your soul warning you to discern before you go all-in.

Do not ever feel pressured to buy into what someone else is selling you. If the "sell-by date" has been changed just because they want to move the product, then the only person who loses out is the customer.

Look to the next passage for more on this...

THIS LITTLE LIGHT OF MINE

This little light of mine, that I had learned to shine, has taken me on a journey inward to serve me. You see, I had heard about this light that could shine so bright, yet I never knew how close it truly was.

I had thought that only other people who were enlightened, like the gurus of this world, could gift me with a light for myself. This is where I began to seek outside of my own being for something that was already there.

I was young, and so naive that I never understood how my own light was already shining brightly. You see, the guru never told me how to make it shine. He only told me that it was up to me to do so, but when? It seemed that the guru had made the pathway towards enlightenment elusive and vague.

This cast a shadow of doubt within my own mind and upon my own path, and where I continued to stand on the sidelines, believing that I would never find it. I watched in awe and wonder as the light of others inspired me. All the while there was a yearning from within me, intuitively reminding me that I had to find my own light, but how?

How could I be like them and encompass such beauty, such wisdom, such knowledge?

How could I become like the beacon of light that they were so perfect at projecting?

I was not able to see my own inner beauty just yet, and so I settled in for the long haul. I settled into a place beneath the shadow of the light that the guru encompassed, not realizing that I was in fact dimming my own light. This little light of mine had not yet found a way to shine, or had it?

Had this internal light of wisdom already begun to shine, and I was just too blind to see it?

Had this light which I had need of already amplified within me?

Was fear standing at the gateway to my own inner peace?

What was the guru not telling me? What was the secret he was keeping from me that could make me shine as he did?

So many questions with so few answers, yet I kept moving on. I sat within the circle of light and love, just wishing that my time would come. I was hoping in some tiny way that I could shine like the guru did, but I doubted in my own ability to do so. I began to think that this was the way of the world and that only the chosen few were illuminated. My disbelief in myself kept me from realizing my own capacity to do the same and more. It was during this time that a shift occurred, and an awakening began presenting itself to me. Was this what I had hoped for?

Had I found the pathway to my own illumination? I stayed the course.

You see, I sat beneath the umbrella of humility and began to share with others what the guru had shared so lovingly with me. The more I shared, the more alive I became. This was where I realized that the guru kept nothing from me and gifted everything to me!

The guru had indeed passed the torch onto me, yet he allowed me to carry it forth in my own perfect timing. This was where I was delivered, through my own voice of wisdom to the light that I had been seeking. You see, the guru had showed me the path, yet he never told me how it should be traveled. He allowed me to discover the light within me by just being the light before me.

The guru was so wise in how he amplified the light within me. He filled my cup daily with wisdom and knowledge. He allowed me to freely drink from this cup when I was thirsty. He knew it was only a matter of time before my cup would overflow and where I would be guided to share what I was taught by him with others. The guru was so wise that he knew it was up to me to see the light. His patience with me was the gift to the seeker of the light that I had become.

This little light of mine, oh, I'm gonna let it shine!

It seems that I had finally found what I had been looking for. Unbeknownst to me, I had been looking in all the wrong places, not yet realizing that nothing external of me was going to be able to fill me. All I needed to do was look inside of myself and everything that I had need of was provided.

It was in this moment that the torch, which had been passed on to me, began to amplify the light within me. The gift from the guru was in the giving, and when I freely received his offering, I became illuminated and began to shine.

Inspired Writing, January 28, 2017

Author's Reflections

This inspired piece was written three months prior to meeting with the man from Peru. I found the story to be helpful and an extension of what was previously written and have decided to add it to this book as a guidepost.

My hopes are that these words become a blueprint for the seekers of their own inner light.

"I AM HEALED, I AM WHOLE, I AM ONE WITH GOD."

This is the mantra that was given to me as a way to assist in the healing that I so desperately needed. The words came to me through the channel of my mediumship; they were shared with me from a voice that was oh so familiar to me. It was 1998, when I made my deal with God. I was sick, I prayed, and I was granted the grace of a healing. I was thirty-four and had a lung condition that could not be diagnosed. I was told by my doctor, that I would need to be on medication and oxygen for the rest of my adult life.

Now let me begin from the beginning…

That year, 1998, I got sick and could not breathe. Tests were run, and I was referred to a pulmonary specialist, who ran his own sets of tests. One day he said to me, "Let's try an experiment," then he took me to the stairwell. He placed an oxygen meter on my finger, and we began running the stairs. With each step, my breathing became more labored, and my oxygen levels fell into the mid-range of 85 to 87.

The doctor scheduled a CT Scan and when the results came back, he said I needed surgery, a biopsy of my lungs. After the results of my scan, I noticed that the doctor seemed to be uneasy at times. Intuitively I felt that he wanted so badly to diagnose my condition, but he could not. Each time I had asked him about it, he just seemed to deflect the question.

All this doctor knew was that the images of the CT Scan showed that my lungs looked like "stained-glass windows." There was no oxygen exchange between the capillaries in my lungs to my bloodstream. This forced me to be on oxygen to survive.

An open lung biopsy was scheduled, which I tried to cancel four days beforehand. With the coaxing from my husband and the surgeon, I agreed to go forward with the procedure. I returned home four days later to await the results. The tissues went to two independent labs and came back with two vastly different interpretations.

One classified my condition as terminal; the other determined that I would need to be on medication and oxygen for life. Perhaps in a show of optimism, the doctor went with the second set of results. He put me on steroids and oxygen and told me he would need to see me again in six weeks.

That same day the nurse stepped in to speak with me in private. She asked, "Do you know what is wrong with you?" When I said no, she replied, "I have copied your medical records for you, and I think you should have them." This made me feel uneasy, as the records showed that my condition had no diagnosis.

This was when I took matters into my own hands and made what I would call my deal with God. I prayed and said, "If You heal me, I will do this for You. The "this" I will not reveal here because it is between me and God. I will say that this was when I became proactive in my own ability to heal myself, with God's help, of course.

The words of Jesus sat with me during this time:

"Your faith has made you well."

I sat every day, at the same time each day, and prayed over myself. I would place my hands over my lungs and breathe deeply. On the exhale I would see the dense energy move out of my lungs; on the inhale, my lungs would be filled with healing purple energy.

It was not long into my new ritual when these words were given to me:

"I am Healed, I am Whole, I am One with God."

They were spoken to me, from what I believe to be the voice of God. I was told that I needed to repeat them during my own healing practices. I continued on with my journey of healing. Each time I sat, I included these words and would speak them over and over again during my thirty-minute sessions.

Six weeks later, I returned to see my doctor. During this time, I had stopped using the oxygen machine and I was feeling like a million bucks. The doctor was astounded when he saw me. He checked my oxygen levels, and they registered at 98%, which was perfect. He told me that he would begin weaning me off the steroids. This was because my lungs were completely clear when he listened to them through the stethoscope.

This is when I told him, *"God helped to heal me."* I explained to him what had happened over those six weeks at home. He smiled at me, shook my hand and said, "Whatever happened here, I am so happy for you." I asked him if it was safe for me to do my open water dive. I had planned a trip to Mexico six months prior to getting sick. He said, "You are cleared to do whatever you would like to do." I was off the next week to vacation with my husband and completed my open water dive in Cancun.

Pretty remarkable what we are each capable of, when we believe, and can see ourselves in perfect health once more. It is from this place where we can become powerful healing advocates for ourselves. It happens when we become active participants in the process.

As Jesus said, "What I can do so can you" ... "Physician heal thyself."

I leave you with this today, as a way to show you that we are each powerful healers in our own right. The power of positive thinking, along with a positive attitude about our current state of affairs, goes a long way in the healing process of self.

Channeled from God and an Inspired True Story May 28, 2017

Author's Reflections

As I reflect on this long-ago miracle it brings me back to something that my teacher Miss Jackie would tell us. She would say, "See yourself in perfect health and so it shall be."

We all have the power to heal aspects of our own lives, even when we are facing an unexpected health crisis. But it is up to us to be proactive in our own healing. Without your own commitment to the journey, the miracle of healing will remain at bay until you call it into action.

It can take a great leap of faith to get into the right mindset, but I believe with God all things are possible.

THE MIRACLE OF THE CHERRY TREE

"When shaking the Cherry Tree Dear Ones, take only that which falls at your feet and leave the rest to ripen. For if you try to pick the fruit before its time, it will never achieve the sweetness that it was destined to reach while remaining on the tree, as its own perfect timing was interrupted and not yet realized."

The cherries are coming in nicely, and each year that I get to harvest this tree's gift, I am reminded of the reason I planted it. I will share with you here a wonderful story, and a tool that you can use as a bridge between yourself and another person.

Through the power of intent and creation within the Universal Mother, she becomes the lightening rod that can help to broker peace and forgiveness between people. She assists you to heal any wounds that you may be carrying within your heart due to conflict you may be having with another.

It was about fifteen years ago, and I was having difficulty getting along with my mother in-law Pat. I was frustrated, hurt, and confused as to why, as I saw it, she was so judgmental of me. Then, one sunny summer day in 2005, I decided to go to the nursery, buy a tree, and plant it as a symbol of peace between us. The cherry tree, then a skinny four-foot sapling, was the one I chose.

I prayed over the tree each time I was near it. I sent this tree all my love, and reiterated my intention to somehow find peace between myself and Pat. Later that same year, a phone call from her turned into a meeting of the minds and hearts. We made amends and never returned to the uncomfortable place we had once been. I thank the cherry tree every time I pass it, for creating a place and a space for my prayer of intent.

Each year that the tree bears fruit, I enjoy the sweetness upon my tongue, and I give thanks to my mother in-law for still being very present in my life, even though she no longer walks among the living.

If you are having difficulty in a relationship, I encourage you to plant something in another person's honor and reap the rewards of your own heartfelt intention. Put all of your love into your planted project. Pray near your own created space of peace and for the peace that you desire. Stay faithful that it will work out in a way that serves you best. In doing so, you will have done your part in the grand scheme of things, and you can move forward in life without being consumed by the wounds of the past.

This is in honor of my mother-in-law, Patricia L. Ninos, who passed away in December of 2013.

Channeled and Inspired Writing June 17, 2017

Author's Reflections

Plant a seed and watch it grow. That is what Jesus taught us as He walked amongst the living. This is where the salve of forgiveness is applied and how the differences between people can find common ground. There is always an open pathway towards forgiveness for each of us, yet we must be opened to its influence.

Jesus taught us that the way to forgiveness is through Unconditional Love. It is a grace for us humans, yet we have to desire it in order for it to be fulfilled.

I share this story with you as a tool to use for yourselves. It is a great way to connect with nature through the planting of something. What you plant does not matter, as the intent behind the planting is what will bear fruit.

I PRAY BECAUSE I AM HUMAN

I pray for myself and others because my faith teaches me to do so.

I pray as a way to find peace within me and for balance within all situations.

I pray to find the answers when I am too deaf to hear and to stubborn to budge.

I pray because I am human.

I pray for myself when I am sick and in need of healing.

I pray for others who are sick and in need of God's Grace.

I pray when I am in despair and in need of God's guidance.

I pray for those who are in need of the same.

I pray because I am human.

I pray in good times and in bad, as prayer becomes my daily ritual.

I pray because it is my connection to source, my connection to God.

I pray because God knows my heart better than I do.

I pray to give thanks when things go my way.

I pray because I am human.

I pray for God's infinite knowledge and wisdom in my daily work and life.

It is through my prayer that I find my humility and realize God's Grace.

I pray that all people can find a place of understanding within their own lives, so that they too can see their way clearly into understanding of who and what they are.

I pray that all people who read these words today can see the power in their own prayerful actions.

I pray today for you, and for me, that all things are made manifest through the prayers of our own intent.

I pray because I am human.

Prayer is a beautiful way to connect at will and when need be. You see, God does not reside in a house or in a church. He resides within each of your own hearts and is easily accessed by just invoking His name.

Inspired Writing, June 14, 2017

Author's Reflections

It is the intent behind your prayers that deliver you to prayer's grace.

Be mindful of that and your prayers will have a defined path to travel.

What you pray for is always answered in unexpected ways. It is in the words used by you, that create the power behind each prayer said.

This is where we honor our human form as we allow prayer to connect us to the God of our own understanding.

PRAYER IS UNIVERSAL IN NATURE

*"The power in prayer happens on a Universal level
when the silent pray.*

*It is the power of the silent voices that change the world
through belief, faith, and hope each day.*

*Prayer becomes the whisper that is carried on the wings
of each Angel today.*

*It is delivered to the places that impact the heart of
humanity in a Universal way.*

*Prayer is Universal in Nature for people
who pray in song.*

*For prayer is received and then given to God's people
when the days feel long.*

*Prayer becomes the healer when the weary are in need.
For prayer is very Universal in every way and deed."*

Channeled on August 16, 2017

Author's Reflections

Those who pray together, like in a church congregation for example, amplify the energy of that prayer so it becomes universal in nature. This is where the heart's desire of many are unified, as they ask for the same thing. This is where they raise their voices in song and in prayer for divine intervention. When we pray Universally and with others, we amplify that prayer ten-fold.

145

In essence, God hears all prayers, and from all people. These prayers are then answered in God's perfect timing.

Have you ever been a part of communal prayer?

How was the power of that communal prayer answered?

Matthew 18:20: "Where two or three are gathered in my name I am in the midst of them."

A moment of reflection would benefit you here.

THE IMAGE OF ONENESS

As I sit here this morning, in the silence of my own mind, immersed in my own surroundings, I feel a sense of peace overcome me.

The feeling is like when one thing shifts away from another, and where I can feel that change is upon me.

It is like a prayer is about to be answered, yet I am also filled with a bit of nervousness about the unknown.

It is that feeling between oh no, and oh yes! But what is it? What news is about to be delivered to me today? Is it good news? Is it bad news? Will it benefit me? These are my questions for right now.

My humanness is in a hurry for the answer. My spirit self, peaking my awareness. My soul, already in alignment for what is to be.

I am in tune with the internal nudges of my own intuition, as my heart tells me the story before the story unfolds in real time.

I have been awakened by the work of self-discovery, as I have allowed my spirit to rise from within me and become a part of my everyday life.

I have moved fully into the oneness of self and all that it encompasses, as flesh and blood become intertwined with the energy of Spirit itself.

I am blessed beyond measure to recognize and know the voice that speaks from within me.

This is what Jesus in my opinion, spoke of when He referenced the Oneness with all that is. That Oneness with the Living God and being in-tune with that divine spark within us. When we become mindful of our own internal nudges is when the Oneness makes its presence known. This is where we can acknowledge it and move in the direction of all that is.

In closing, I feel that this is where the true meaning of *"you complete me"* comes into play, as nothing external of yourself can ever complete the soul's perfection.

Inspired Writing, March 8, 2018

Author's Reflections

Are you searching for that piece of the puzzle, that one single person, that perfect situation to complete you?

If your answer is yes, then I ask you to sit in silence for a moment. This is where you can clear your mind of all thought and sit in the pure energy of your own soul's wisdom. This is where you can connect to the energy of your own spirit and begin to feel the power of your own greatness.

We are taught throughout life that someone or something is needed in order for us to be complete. Whose rules are these and why have we taken them on as our own truth? When we can honestly answer this question, we can then begin to recognize that all we have need of has already been provided.

A great way to connect to the complete part of self is to put on a short piece of music. As you listen, allow yourself to transcend time and space. This is where you can disconnect from the ego's voice that says you are incomplete unless this, that, or the other thing is present. This is where you will find the fullness of the spirit within you and begin to see how completion feels for you.

SLEEP NO MORE

These words spoken by Jesus, *"What I can do, so can you and more"* are placed within the hearts of all people. When Jesus healed the sick, He said, *"Open your eyes and see, stand and walk, heal thyself."* When Jesus spoke the words of God into existence, He did so as a way to awaken all people to God's grace and glory. He was a teacher, a preacher, a prophet and more.

Jesus knew the importance of His ministry, and through His example He showed His disciples the way. This is when Jesus taught them how to connect to the voice of God through prayer in meditation. He did this so that they too could speak from this same place of knowledge. This is where He laid the groundwork for them to teach people to open their hearts to the way long after His death. Jesus taught us that through these avenues, the voice of God is heard by those who are open to His Wisdom.

I write about Jesus at times in my blog and speak about Him and God often to groups of people. Why? Because His life, and ministry speak to my own heart. I know that when I do this, I am speaking from a place of truth within me. I believe that Jesus's gospel was given to us so that we could share it with others as we help to awaken those who sleep.

My work as a medium is driven by my own beliefs, which are:

"It is through God's divine hand where I am guided from."

I have never hidden my love of God and even in my classes, you will often hear me speak about God's influence over my life. I am guided to believe that we are all driven from an internal perspective to do the work that our soul was born to do. This may not be popular with everyone, and judgement may land at your doorstep. It is for you to sweep it away as you stay true to who you are.

I have had opinions given to me by others as I share through these avenues. I have been told that I am doing the work of the Devil and that people have asked their pastors to pray for me. I am never offended by this at all, and to be honest with you, it makes me chuckle. It just perplexes me at times as to why they feel this way about people who speak from a place of truth within them. I can see how even in the twenty-first century Jesus's gospel still creates a stir among the faithful and in the hearts of the non-believers.

I credit this to the ego of man. It is the ego that becomes the veil, which at times can overshadow the light from within. When the ego is out of step with the light, things like judgment, persecution, and negativity can pour from people like a spicket of water fully opened. To me this goes against the grain of what Jesus came back to teach all men and women, which is,

"Judge not lest ye be Judged."

In the end, I know that we can only be responsible for ourselves as we stay true to our own heart's desire. For me, it is a testament to the teachings of Christ, yet I know that I am still a human being, flaws, and all.

Today this is where I find my peace. I know that those who have need of what I have to offer will eat from my table as we share a common bond within a world of many.

This is where a thread of light connects us on a heart level and where we learn to empower one another. This is where we will each awaken, in our own perfect timing, and we will do so one day at a time.

Inspired Writing, April 23, 2018

SLEEP NO MORE

Author's Reflections

Are you a person who cares about what others think of you? Or do you like to color outside of the lines? I would say that we all want to be accepted and it can hurt when we are rejected for our beliefs.

In life, Jesus was a trailblazer, and He connected the dots for us towards God. As we can see, it was not always an easy road for Him to travel yet He stayed true to His purpose.

The same can be said for those who step outside of the colored lines today. It can cause a stir in the hearts of those who are still frightened to do so for themselves. This is where people tend to judge and at times ridicule others for shining a bright light in a dark place.

All I can say is this: you will know when it is your own time to shine and the need to be accepted by everyone else will just fall away. This is where you will see that those who thirst for what you have to say, will drink from your well of knowledge. This is when you will see that your purpose has a place within a world of many.

"It is the brave who will blaze a trail in order for others to find the courage to do the same for themselves, yet it is not the brave who validate you. It is the willingness of the brave to do what others are not yet ready to do that will cause a stir within another's heart. This is how the brave help to ignite the light within those who are ready to do the same thing."

Validation of self is where your power resides!!!

HEAVEN SENT

Man versus Spirituality, Heaven versus Hell.

I found myself reading the obituaries today – family and friends sharing heartfelt moments and memories with strangers in a newspaper; people like you and me, reading about those who we do not know. It got me thinking about the concept of "Heaven."

What is Heaven really, and why are some people drawn to the word while others are repelled by it?

A lot of people will tell you that Heaven is a term made up by religions to brainwash you into behaving according to their rules. If you are good you go to Heaven; if you are bad you go to Hell. These same people will tell you that the bible is a made-up book, and that nothing you read within it is true. They will tell you that it was written or altered to fit the powerful's agenda.

Now others will tell you, wholeheartedly, that they believe in Heaven and that this is the place where you will go when God calls you home. These same people live by the principles written within the bible, because they know the words to be gospel for themselves. This gospel becomes the truth, which is burned into their hearts and minds. It is from the words in the scripture that they have built a foundation on which to stand. They resonate deeply with the passages and draws from them a sense of understanding and direction.

As for me, I believe in what is called Heaven, yet I also feel the word Heaven was "Heaven-sent" if you will.

I believe that the word Heaven was gifted to us and given by God as a way for us to gain a sense of time and space. We can choose to recognize Heaven as a place where our loved ones will be waiting for us when we cross the great divide.

The Kingdom of Heaven is the place that Jesus spoke of in the gospel. He tells us that we will be granted eternal life once we are no longer made of flesh and blood. It is my belief that we are all granted eternal life due to Jesus's sacrifice for us. It is my faith in the words of the scripture that guides my belief. But some people need something tangible to believe in, as they feel a deep separation from that Oneness with God.

Heaven is what I would refer to as the "Spirit World," the place where the soul returns to when their human existence has expired.

What do you believe "Heaven" is?

Take a moment to sit with this question. Allow yourself the opportunity to connect with yourself on a deeper level and feel where the answer to this question resides for you. There is no right or wrong answer here, there is just a place within you that will resonate with your own personal truth.

Inspired Writing August 2, 2018

Author's Reflections

What are your own beliefs when it comes to Heaven and how do you resonate deeply with them today?

Sit with that for a moment. See if your beliefs of yesterday are different from where you find your beliefs moving toward today. This will tell you a lot about your individual growth.

Throughout our lifetime we will all change course when it comes to our beliefs. We gain new perspectives daily, and when they speak our language, we will take them on as our own truth. This becomes evident of our own evolution on a personal level.

See how the words of yesterday become the foundation of your today.

ENLIGHTENMENT THROUGH THE WAY ENCOMPASSES SPIRITUALITY

"Buddha came to teach Enlightenment."

"The Christ came to teach the Way."

"The Tao was born of both aspects."

"One teaches how to navigate Spirituality; one teaches how to navigate Mankind; and the other teaches how to navigate the Natural World. All applied together will teach you how to navigate the human existence through spirituality, and where the human being finds himself in the natural world today."

Channeled by The Council of Nine August 8, 2018

Author's Reflections

I like to call this "The Big Three." They each teach us how to navigate them in one way, shape or form. The channeled information is clear and allows you to see how one road leads to another and so forth.

IN GOD WE TRUST

I woke up in the middle of this night to these powerful words:

"God will never let you down as He always has a hand extended to you when you need to be lifted up."

I thought to myself, *Wow that is powerful,* and as always, I said thank you. I needed to hear that on this night, as I had a few heavy things on my mind during this time.

Each night, before I close my eyes, I always pray for my friends and family. It is my ritual. When I see them struggling in life, I call upon a few extra favors in their honor before I lay my own head down to rest. It is when things feel hopeless that I invoke the power of prayer. It always seems to bring me a sense of peace.

The guidance given to me about prayer has always been:

"When you pray for another person, their own soul is elevated towards the light."

This to me, is what the power of prayer means on a grand scale and gives me comfort. Intuitively I know this is the only control that I have over any given situation.

We all want to help out those closest to us and we forget sometimes that it is not up to us to fix them, but we can always pray for them.

For today, if you want to help someone out from the sidelines, I encourage you to use the power of prayer. This is where your requests for that person are heard on a universal level, and where miracles can happen each and every day.

I like to believe that a few kind words in favor of another go a long way.

Channeled and Inspired Writing, August 16, 2018

Author's Reflections

The comfort in this message is that,

"God will never let you down as He always has a hand extended to you, when you need to be lifted up."

All you have to do is trust in Him and reach for that hand. This is where you put your faith in front of your fears and allow a space to be opened up within you.

Let me ask you this:

Where has God lifted you up in life, or even those you have prayed for?

Reflecting on this question will show you the Glory of God's Grace in motion. This is when your hearts are opened to His will and where you can find peace in any difficult situation.

PRAYER FOR PEACE

"Words of Peace Spoken...Energy Transmuted...and from Darkness arises the Light...

Each Soul, each Person has a duty while living a human lifetime. That duty is to be mindful of their words, peaceful in their thoughts and to understand the Evolution of this Planet and its People.

Never underestimate the Power of your Words, for what you Speak into existence today will become a Tangible Energy, which then takes on a Life of its Own. Peace to you Dear Ones."

A s I sit with this channeled message, I recognize the truth of it on a universal level.

I understand that as we move into this Age of Aquarius, that old paradigms are fighting hard to stop the natural progression of change.

I can see words of hate being spoken, people being taken advantage of by the powerful, and the light fighting its way through the darkness.

I can see where the words spoken by others have become a tangible energy and have taken on a lifeforce of their own.

When I think of the word "peace," I understand its place within my own life and how peace is an individual journey of the soul.

It is up to the human being to find a sense of peace within their own lives before peace can make an impact upon the world around them.

159

This is after all, what Jesus was trying to teach.

So, for today, I send out a prayer that "peace" finds its way into the hearts of those in need of its compassion, and where its impact is felt Universally.

Channeled and Inspired Writing, November 30, 2018

Author's Reflections

Words contain the power of creation, and when we tap into old patterns of behavior, we then allow the past to become fully present in our lives today.

Our words become like old paradigms as they try to stay relevant in our evolution.

Shatter the patterns of the past and give space to evolve into the new you.

DIVINE PIECES OF GOD'S LIGHT

*"You are all divine pieces of God's Light walking
individual paths of purpose."*

I write this after seeing a question posed by a teacher to a group of people. It went something like this:

When did Jesus go from being a "man" to being "Divine"?

I have given it quite a bit of thought, and I would answer it this way.

We are all divine, just as Jesus was. As I see it, our purpose is individual to the life that we are living right now. Jesus was most definitely born a physical man. His job was to teach the people with purpose. He lived as an example for humanity so He could awaken the world to God's Light.

He was known to say; *"The Kingdom of God is within you,"* hence the awakening part of His mission.

Now, in each century there have been many who set an example through the life they were living. Some did this on a smaller scale than others, but they were examples, nonetheless.

There is one example that comes to mind for me as I reflect here today. Princess Diana married into a family that could place her in the spotlight. This gave her the power to realize her purpose from a bigger platform. It was from this platform that we each saw her purpose fulfilled in real time.

Diana lived a life of royalty, but it was her compassion that became evident to all people. Her purpose, through compassion, touched those whom she could reach through the example of the life she was living. She had a deep love for children, and she used her place of prominence to help underprivileged sick babies and kids.

Her compassion towards people who were ill made them feel like they were whole again when in her presence. Her desire was to care for and feed the poor. She did this as a way to shine a light on who some would call the forgotten men, women, and children of this world. This was when her purpose was on full display.

Princess Diana was not afraid to walk among the sick; in fact, like Jesus, she even touched them with her bare hands. It was in the 1980s when AIDS was running rampant, and along with it came fear and stigma. Princess Diana taught us through her actions, by using physical touch, to defy the ignorance of people and laying fear to rest. This is only one of many examples of a single woman, who lived a royal life, and used her position in life to do good work. Her mission as I see it, is in alignment with what Jesus did during His own time on earth.

The connection through love, compassion, and prayer tied this woman to the work of Christ. It was her humility that endeared her to the hearts of millions. Her life while short, served a great purpose, and her purpose was in alignment with humanity. In essence, Princess Diana was able to shine a light on fear so that it could be replaced with love.

The beauty of purpose being displayed from this woman as I see it, was to awaken the world from her platform of individuality. The divine plan of the soul before it is born into the physical world is masterful. All things are in alignment with its destined path; all things are governed by the Light of God, Universal Laws, and Free Will.

Who do you think of as an influential person who walked a path of purpose? Who is it that you see as a world-changer who had set their sights on the movement of "Awakening"?

These are the questions to be pondered as we move more fully into the Age of Aquarius and experience Jesus in the twenty-first century.

Channeled and Inspired Writing, November 15th, 2019

Author's Reflections

What and who are you in alignment with and how have they become an example for you to follow?

This is a big question, as it lends credence to your own purposeful movements and actions in this lifetime. What difference do you want to make in this world that encompasses the good of all and not just for the good of self?

HE IS THE WAY

"It is through the Light that the Way has been Illuminated, and it is from this place of Love, that He lived and where He died for your sins."

In today's world, Christians still celebrate the Life of Christ. We have been taught to believe that it is through Him that we will be granted Everlasting Life.

In John 10:27–29 Jesus states that: My sheep hear my voice, and I know them, and they follow me; I give unto them eternal life; and they shall never perish; and My Father, who has given them to me, is greater than all, no one can snatch them out of my Father's hand.

The beauty of the written word is that it is interpreted by each human being in a way that becomes meaningful for them.

Channeled and Inspired Writing, November 15, 2020

Author's Reflections

Take the written word and consume it. Allow it to fill you up so that you can see what it means to be full.

SIN

"Sin is a Stain on the Soul and through the Grace of Everlasting Life that has been promised to you through the Sacrifice of Jesus, your sins are washed away."

As humans we navigate a world of many in order to learn, yet God asks us to grow in Him. The beauty of bringing the Christ Light into your own self is that you allow others to see the Christ Light within themselves through your example.

"Be the Reflection of what you desire to see in others. Those who are ready to Embrace the Reflection of His Love will then see in all places, His Grace."

Inspired and Channeled, December 3, 2020

Author's Reflections

As this book draws to a close, we find ourselves here together in the reflection of the Christ. This moment is a great time to take a look at your own reflection now, and where I humbly ask you this...

Where have the ripples of your own example touched the lives of others?

It is in the ripples, from a single pebble tossed, that will touch the shoreline in an impactful way.

AFTERWORD

I would like to close this book of wisdom with words that have been inspired through me. They come with the assistance of my Council, as they help us to understand the rituals created and used as a gateway towards the God of our own understanding.

Rituals become the Pathway

I am often asked; how do you pray and invoke God daily?

I begin each day with a prayer of intent, created from a place within me and for myself. I use words that invoke my connection to God, open me up to communications with my Council, which brings me into alignment with my purpose.

My students always ask me to teach them how to speak my prayer of intent so that they too can create a link to their own divine purpose. I always encourage them to add any words to this prayer that will serve them in their daily lives. This way, I know that they can take what they have learned from me now and make it their own.

As I have been guided to understand, we are all born so that we can learn from one another. The one thing I hope I can teach you here is about the power of prayer. I pray because my spirit calls me to. My prayer speaks to the heart of my own internal truth. I pray as a way to extend my deep gratitude to God and for His love of me.

I know that through my purpose I am the amplifier of the light within others. I know that I am a port of light in a sea of many. I know that my purpose is to share what the Spirit World has so beautifully shared with me. I know that my purpose serves me well.

Today is the day to find the passion in your own spirit and

invoke that beautiful purpose to make its presence known. Say a prayer of intent daily and call into your life what you have need of. Please remember that it is through the simple path that you are fed, yet it is up to you to step upon that path to awaken the sleeping parts of you.

Enjoy this prayer and please add the words that will serve you best as you find a way to make it your own.

Dear God,

Surround and fill my physical being with the pure Christ Light of perfect love and protection. Keep me safe from harmful, evil, and negative influences as I float in the sea of Your divine love.

At this time, I call upon all of my master guides and teachers, beings of light, and my guardian angel from God. This is where I seek Your guidance.

I ask that my inner light shine bright for all of the world to see, so that I may be the amplifier of the light within others.

I ask that I become a clear channel for all divine information to flow through. For those who need to hear my words, I ask that they may find their way to my table.

I ask that God's divine hand guide me daily as I navigate a world of many. In Jesus name, I pray. Amen.

Inspired Writing December 14, 2020

May God Bless your life and your journey as we all navigate this world of many.

CONTINUE YOUR JOURNEY
WITH MEDIUM PATTY HORTON

Thank you for reading my book. It has been an honor to share the written word with each of you here. If you would like to continue to journey with me, I have included links to my guided meditations for your enjoyment. They can be purchased through the streaming service of your choice. Scroll down to read about my free gift!!!

Awaken to the Beauty of your Own Inner Light 2015

https://music.apple.com/us/album/awaken-to-beauty-your-own-inner-light-guided-meditation/1005017114

Reflections of Body, Mind, Spirit 2017

https://www.amazon.com/Reflections-Body-Spirit-Guided-Meditation/dp/B01MS4KNXU

Journey into the Magic Mirror 2020

https://mediumpattyhorton.hearnow.com/journey-into-the-magic-mirror

Connect with me at my website and enjoy one of my many services offered.

https://www.innereyeconnections.com

***Mediumship Reading

***Mentorship Program

***Ask Patty

For those of you who become subscribers, I would like to give you a gift.

I will send you the audio download to my White Light Guided Meditation once your subscription is verified.

Click on the Gmail link and in the subject line write Subscribe. When your subscription is verified, you will be forwarded the audio download.

pattyscrystalball@gmail.com

ABOUT THE AUTHOR

Patty Horton is a medium, trance medium, spiritual teacher, author, and mentor who helps to educate the spiritually curious. She teaches people how to connect with their own intuition and guides them to explore their divine gifts. She introduces them to the language of the soul.

Patty's philosophy is to keep it simple, which is how the Spirit World has encouraged her to teach. It is from this platform that all people are fed from her own place of knowledge and understanding; it is also why with her thirty-nine years of experience she is known as one of the most insightful mediums and spiritual teachers of our day.

Patty reads from a channeled perspective and teaches from a place of experience. Her passion for this work is evident to those who sit before her for a reading or within the walls of her classroom. People take comfort in her presence due to Patty's own understanding of her place upon the path. She wears a cloak of humility upon her shoulders when doing this work. This is where she opens the doorway and extends an invitation to Spirit's influence and gives them a space to explore the divine light within you.

In the words of her Council.

"The Spirit World will always give to you what you have need of, for we can see the greatest good and highest joy of each soul that we are working with."

For more information on Patty Horton please visit her website:

www.innereyeconnections.com

CPSIA information can be obtained
at www.ICGtesting.com
Printed in the USA
FSHW020318101121
86020FS